A BOOK OF
POT-POURRI

A BOOK OF
POT-POURRI

New and Old Ideas for
Fragrant Flowers and Herbs

GAIL DUFF

ILLUSTRATED BY
CHERRY DENMAN

BEAUFORT BOOKS
Publishers
New York

For My Mother

Designed and produced by Breslich & Foss, London
Designer: Roger Daniels
Editor: Monique Maxwell

Text © Gail Duff 1985
Illustrations © Cherry Denman 1985

Library of Congress Cataloging in Publication Data

Duff, Gail.
   A book of pot-pourri

   Includes index.
   1. Handicraft.   I. Denman, Cherry.   II. Title.
TT157. D82 1985 745.5.   84-28316
ISBN 0-8253-0296-X

Published in the United States by
Beaufort Books Publishers. New York

Printed in Spain by SIRVEN GRAFIC, Barcelona
First American edition

10 9 8 7 6 5 4 3 2 1

The author and publisher are satisfied that the
recipes in this book are safe and effective.
However, they cannot be held responsible for any
adverse consequences resulting from the use or
misuse of these recipes.

CONTENTS

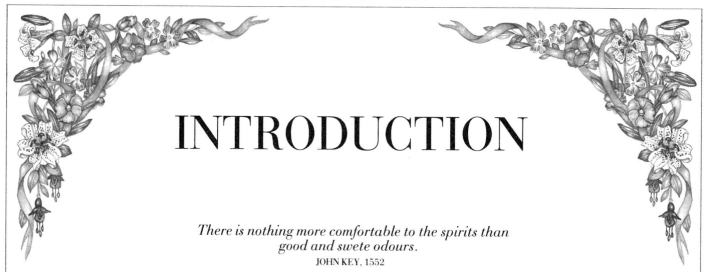

INTRODUCTION

There is nothing more comfortable to the spirits than
good and swete odours.
JOHN KEY, 1552

What a barren world this would be without the sweet, natural scents of herbs and flowers. For many centuries they have enhanced gardens, improved living conditions, kept away disease, relieved depression and aroused passions.

The ancient Egyptians used scented oils for massage, washed royal barges with scented water and preserved rose-petals by burying them in crocks. The Greeks and Romans strewed flowers in front of processions and over banqueting halls, and used scented preparations in the baths for which they were famous.

And then the slaves brought water for the hands
And soap mix'd with oily juice of lilies,
and poured o'er the hands as much warm water
as the guests wished. An then they gave them towels
of finest linen, beautifully wrought,
and fragrant ointments of ambrosial smell,
and garlands of the flow'ring violet.

In Saxon Britain, the monks spent many hours tending herbs in their monastery gardens later using them in preparations to heal the sick. In medieval times, it was well recognised that flower scents were therapeutic.

The still room became an essential part of every house in the sixteenth century. Here, the lady of the house and her servants would take their freshly-gathered flowers and herbs, dry them, distil them and make them into sweet waters, medicines, pomanders and sweet bags.

It is hard to imagine life in those times: houses were often damp and musty-smelling, there was no sanitation, people rarely washed and disease was rife. Instead of abolishing unpleasant smells altogether, they were simply masked by the pleasant: bowls of dried and cured flowers were placed about the house, bedrooms were fumigated, bunches of herbs and sachets of spices were placed in the linen chest, pomanders were carried in times of plague. Heady scents were everywhere.

However, even as sanitation and cleanliness increased, still room work was just as essential for there was no other way of combatting illness and imported perfumes and scents were expensive. Besides this, what a delightful way to spend your time: pounding and mixing and testing the scents, going out into the garden and picking roses, tending herbs and then putting the sweetly-scented preparations to good use. One imagines a warm, airy, sweetly-scented room with ladies in eighteenth-century dress calmly and expertly going about their tasks. The old recipes may seem obscure with their instructions to 'use as much as you think fit' and 'take a handful' of some ingredient, but these ladies were far more familiar with methods for using herbs in the kitchen than we are today.

Compared to past centuries, our way of life today is rather sterile. True, we have abolished all the unpleasant smells, but do we really give enough time to the pleasant? We need to relax in sweetly-scented surroundings, to grow and care

for useful plants. Their transient and delicate scents can comfort, calm and uplift. Herbalists in the past have written about this; recent research has proved it.

Today, we can buy beauty preparations, fresh air sprays and moth repellants. Some smell tolerable, many rather awful and there is little pleasure to be found in purchasing them from the supermarket. If we can spare the time, we should make at least some of these ourselves. It is so much more satisfying, and when working on them one gets something of the feeling of the old still room. You mix and stir, look (sometimes with satisfied amazement) at the effect, add a few drops of flower oil or some chopped herbs and smell; it takes you back to a summer garden.

Of course, if you grow your own herbs and flowers, so much the better, but if you have not so much as a window box, do not despair for there are many good herbalists around now and some have very comprehensive mail order lists.

Pot-pourri, a mixture of flowers, herbs, spices and aromatic oils, has come to symbolise the products of the still room. This is *A Book of Pot-Pourri*, not because it is devoted entirely to making bowls full of this fragrant mixture, but because it is in itself a pot-pourri. It contains a mixture of ideas for making the best use of fragrant flowers or herbs, whether you simply wish to sit in a scented garden or to fill your house with the fragrant products of your still room.

Herbs do comfort the wearied braine with fragrant smells which yield a certain kinde of nourishment.

WILLIAM COLES,
1656

If odours may worke satisfaction, they are so soveraigne in plants and so comfortable that no confection of the apothecaries can equall their excellent virtue.

JOHN GERARD,
1597

I would heartily advise all men of meanes, to be stirred up to bend their mindes, and spend a little more time and travell in these delights of herbes and flowers, than they have formerly done, which are not only harmlesse, but pleasurable in their turn, and profitable in their use.

PARKINSON, 1640

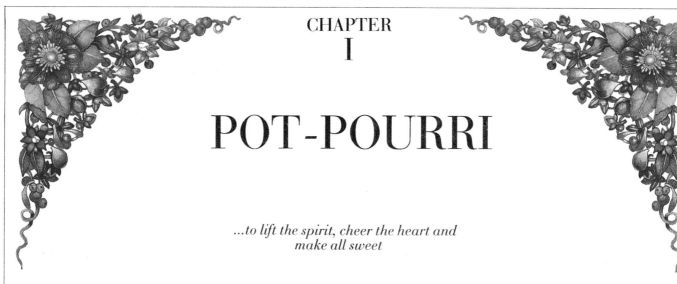

CHAPTER
I

POT-POURRI

*...to lift the spirit, cheer the heart and
make all sweet*

ORIGINS

The term pot-pourri has come to mean the mixtures of dried flowers and herbs, plus spices and other fragrant ingredients which are kept in open bowls or perforated containers to gently and subtly perfume a room

If 'pot-pourri' is literally translated from the French, it means 'rotten pot', and this refers to the original way of making it; fresh or semi-dried flowers and petals would be layered in a crock with salt to cure or ferment them, thus preserving an exceptionally strong and long-lasting scent.

This method of preserving summer flowers to provide scent in winter was originally used by the ancient Egyptians and Greeks who buried crocks of fresh rose petals for later use.

Pot-pourri making did not become popular in Britain until the sixteenth century when spices for underlying fragrance and ingredients for fixing the scent became more widely available. The finished mixtures were kept in bowls. In small houses with high windows, damp, and beaten mud floors, they were essential for sweetening the air.

...And how well I remember the sweet, subdued scent of pot-pourri, for as well as flowers there were in every room big open bowls of the pot-pourri she loved to have about her.

ELEANOR SINCLAIR-RHODE,
The Scented Garden, c.1920

The sharper scented herbs such as lavender, rosemary and southernwood which were added to them also helped to keep away infection.

By the eighteenth century, many different recipes for pot-pourri had been written and experimented with and most country ladies had their own special formula which had been handed down through generations. Instead of 'rotten pot' the mixture made by layering with salt was known by the more evocative name of 'Sweet Jar'.

Today, pot-pourri can be made using either the dry method (p 21) or the moist method (p 25). Once the basic ingredients have become familiar and the few easy rules learned, the combinations of flowers, herbs and spices that can be put together are infinite. They can be made relaxing or activating, refreshing or sensual, whichever you choose.

No bought pot-pourri is so pleasant as that made from one's own garden, for the petals of the flowers one has gathered at home hold the sunshine and memories of summer, and of past summers only the sunny days should be remembered.

ELEANOR SINCLAIR-RHODE, *The Scented Garden*, c.1920

INGREDIENTS

Flowers

Sweet-scented rose petals have always been the most important ingredient in a moist pot-pourri, and they nearly always form the base of a pot-pourri made by mixing completely dried ingredients. However, there are other flowers suitable for both the moist and dry methods of preparing a pot-pourri: Bergamot, Carnations, Heliotrope, Honeysuckle, Jonquil, Lavendar, Lilac, Lily of the Valley, Lime flowers, Mignonette, Mock Orange Blossom, Nicotiniana, Orange Blossom, Peony, Pinks, Roman Camomile, Stocks, Violets, and Wallflowers.

Herbs and leaves

As well as flowers, herbs and leaves play an important role in making a fragrant pot-pourri. Lavender, rosemary, marjoram, thyme and woodruff, for example, all become more fragrant when dried. Lemon verbena was an extremely popular addition to the pot-pourri:

I have never known anyone, not even those who dislike strongly scented flowers, not to be delighted with the delicious smell of its leaves, which they retain long after they are dried.

MRS. EARLE, *Pot-Pourri from a Scented Garden*, 1905

Other herbs and leaves that can be used include: Agrimony, Bay, Basil, Bergamot, Bergamot Mint, Birch Buds, Calamint, Clary Sage, Costmary, Cotton Lavender, Geraniums (Sweet scented varieties), Germander, Lemon

Dry roses put to the nose to smell do comfort the Brayne and the herte and quickeneth the spryte.

ASKHAM'S HERBAL, 1550

The rose looks fair, but fairer we it deem for that sweet odour that in it doth live

SHAKESPEARE

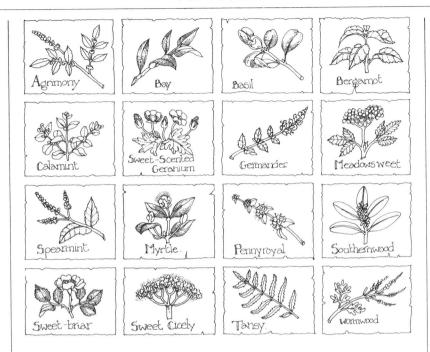

Balm, Meadow Sweet, Mints (Eau-de-Cologne, Apple, Spearmint), Myrtle, Pennyroyal, Pineapple Sage, Santolina, Southernwood, Sweet Briar, Sweet Cicely, Tansy, Verbena, and Wormwood.

Colour

As well as being fragrantly-scented, a pot-pourri should be attractive to look at. When dried, many herbs and petals fade and become more uniform in colour. If the pot-pourri is eventually to be kept in an open bowl or glass container, add dried white or brightly-coloured flowers to improve its appearance. The following are especially effective: Baby's Breath, Bergamot, Borage, Cornflower, Delphinium, Forget-Me-Not, Hydrangeas, Larkspur, Marigolds, Nasturtiums, Pansies, petals of Daisy-shaped flowers, Red Cardinal flowers, Salvia, Tansy, and Zinnias.

Spices

Besides the flowers and herbs which give a pot-pourri its main scent, spices, woods and citrus peels are usually added to give a more full-bodied scent.

Those spices most commonly used in pot-pourri are the sweet spices such as cinnamon, cassia, cloves, allspice, nutmeg and occasionally mace. Ginger and carraway or fennel seeds can be mixed with these spices and, to give a faint Oriental scent, anise, coriander and cardamon also.

Spices for a moist or dry pot-pourri should be either coarsely ground in a mill or pounded in a mortar. Powdered spices quickly lose their scent and spoil the appearance of a dry pot-pourri if it is put into a glass container by sticking to the glass and making it cloudy. Whole cloves or small pieces of whole mace, cinnamon stick and cassia can make a dry pot-pourri more attractive. Add them after the crushed spices have been mixed into the other ingredients.

Successful spice combinations include:

CINNAMON, CASSIA, CLOVES, MACE

CINNAMON, ALLSPICE, NUTMEG, CARAWAY

CARDAMON, CORIANDER, ANISE, CARAWAY

CARDAMON, CINNAMON, ANISE, FENNEL

CLOVES, ALLSPICE, MACE, CASSIA

Woods

Scented wood has long been recognised as most appealing to the senses, as suggested in the song:

Quinquereme of Nineveh from distant Ophir,
Rowing home to haven in sunny Palestine,
With a cargo of ivory
And apes and peacocks,
Sandalwood, and cedarwood, and sweet white wine.

Those that are available in the form of powder or scrapings include:

SANDALWOOD
sharp and bitter scent

CEDAR
pinelike and antiseptic

SANTAL
warm and sweet

SASSAFRAS
spicy

Citrus peel

In many old pot-pourri recipes, dried whole oranges are crushed and mixed in with the spices.

To achieve a similar effect, thinly pare the rind from an orange or lemon, rub the pieces with orris root, and lay them on a cake cooling rack. Dry them in a low oven (200°F, 100°C) until crisp. They can be added to pot-pourri mixtures whole or crushed.

For a more spicy scent, push a clove through each piece of peel before drying.

Fixatives

Even when flowers have been dried correctly their scents are very transient. Adding a fixative will help to preserve the highly volatile plant oils.

Early pot-pourri makers used fixatives of animal origin, such as musk, ambergris and civet. These are not always obtained through humane methods, and it is now best to use plant alternatives:

ORRIS ROOT: This is the most readily available fixative and one which has been used for centuries with great success. It is the dried root of *Iris florentina*, and besides fixing the scents of other flowers it has a gentle violet scent of its own. It is most commonly available ground, in the form of a white powder. The scent of whole pieces is stronger, but these are extremely hard and difficult to crush or grate.

GUM BENZOIN: In many old recipes this is referred to as benjamin. It is the resin of the tree Styrax benzoin and can be bought as a ground, grey-brown gum, or in the form of a tincture.

CALAMUS POWDER: This is the dried, ground root of the sweet flag, *Acorus calamus*.

COUMARIN: This is the ingredient in woodruff and meadow-sweet which makes them smell like new-mown hay. The leaves of these plants themselves added to a pot-pourri will help to fix the scents of other flowers.

TONQUIN OR TONKA BEANS: These also contain coumarin and have a vanilla-like scent.

VETEVIER: This is a sweet-smelling grass, the root of which is occasionally used as a fixative. It can be bought as shreds or scrapings, or as an essential oil. The scent is something between orris root and sandalwood.

SANDALWOOD: Either scrapings or powder will fix other scents, besides adding the sharp one of sandalwood. Alternatively, sandalwood oil can be used.

PATCHOULI: This is an Indian plant with a musky, woody smell. It is very strong, so use only a little. It is available in leaf, powder or oil form.

MYRRH AND FRANKINCENSE: These are little used now, but can be bought in the form of powder or grains. They are the gum resins of sweet-scented trees.

When using old recipes which include animal fixatives, substitute the following plant fixatives: *for civet:* orris root or vetevier; *for musks:* patchouli, amberette seeds, angelica root, moss roses, oil of musk, or rose; *for ambergris:* sandalwood. All of these, apart from patchouli, need a further fixative.

Essential oils

Essential oils are usually added to dry pot-pourri mixtures to strengthen the scent. Oils are available from a wide range of scented plants, but their strength and quality can vary.

Ready-mixed pot-pourri oils, both natural and chemical, are also available. Oil should be added to pot-pourri mixtures drop by drop, mixed in well, and tested for scent before any more is added. Should you wish to double the amount of ingredients in a recipe, add a different oil rather than more of the given one; this will prevent the scent from being too overpowering.

Salt

Salt is used as a preservative when making moist pot-pourri. It prevents decay and keeps away insects.

Bay salt was stipulated in most old recipes. Now it is best to use non-iodised sea salt. Have a mixture of equal parts of coarse and fine and dry it in a low oven for several hours before use.

HARVESTING AND DRYING

Of their sweet death are sweetest odours made.
SHAKESPEARE

Roses should always be gathered just before they are fully open, as once they are full-blown both scent and colour will diminish when they are dried. Gather them on a dry day, after the dew has dried, but before the hot, noon sun makes the garden smell of roses. Pick only perfect blooms and pull off the petals away from direct sunlight.

Other sweet-scented flowers should be gathered just as they begin to open. Cut sprigs of herbs just before the flowers appear.

To prevent mildew, petals and leaves should be dried as quickly as possible, but they should never be exposed to strong sun or too great a heat. A warm, dry, airy room is ideal.

Petals and flowers should be spread out to dry on racks. These can be made by stretching muslin over light wooden frames. Cover the flowers with kitchen paper or more muslin raised on upturned egg cups or glasses so that it does not touch the flowers.

Herbs can be laid uncovered on the racks, or hung up in small bunches.

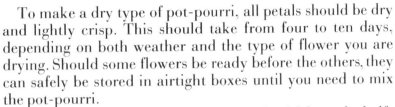

You must in rose-time make choice of such roses as are neither in the bud, nor full blowne which you must specially cull and chuse from the rest, then take sand and dry it thoroughly well, and having shallow boxes, make first an even lay of sand, upon which lay your rose-leaves one by one (so as none of them touch other). Set this box in some warme, sunny place in a hot sunny day (and commonly in two hot sunny dayes they will be thorow dry), and thus you may have rose-leaves and other flowers to lay about your basons, windows, etc., all winter long.

SIR HUGH PLATT, *Delights for Ladies*, 1594

To make a dry type of pot-pourri, all petals should be dry and lightly crisp. This should take from four to ten days, depending on both weather and the type of flower you are drying. Should some flowers be ready before the others, they can safely be stored in airtight boxes until you need to mix the pot-pourri.

For a moist pot-pourri, the petals should be only half-dried and leathery. This takes about two days; those dry first can be stored until the rest are ready.

MAKING A POT-POURRI
BY THE DRY METHOD

Take of orris root, sweet calamus, cypress root, dried lemon peel and dried orange peel of each a pound; a peck [2 gallons] of dried rose petals. Make all except rose petals into a gross powder, then take coriander seeds 4 ounces, nutmegs 1½ oz and cloves 1 ounce and mix with the other when powdered. Then add musk and ambergris 15 grains [15 pinches] mixed. Then take 4 large handfuls of lavender dried and freed from the stalks, of sweet marjoram, orange petals and young walnut leaves 1 handful each all dried. Mix together and place in bits of cotton perfumed with essences.

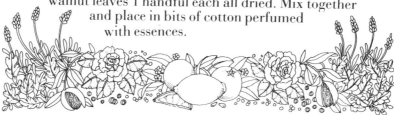

The dry type of pot-pourri is the easiest to make and the final result is prettier than the moist type since all the petals and leaves remain separate and intact. The natural scents of the flowers, however, are not so well preserved as with the moist method, so essential oils have to be added for extra fragrance.

Ingredients

Rose petals are the main ingredient in many dry pot-pourris, either alone or mixed with other sweet-smelling flowers. Herbs, spices and citrus peels are added in smaller amounts to give a more full-bodied perfume.

A dry pot-pourri can also be made without rose petals. It can for example be based on a mixture of carnations, lilac, violets and wallflowers for a sweet scent, or on lavender for one that is fresh and clean. A 'green' pot-pourri based on lemon verbena and other herbs is sharp and invigorating. Scented geranium leaves can also be used as a base.

Dessicants

To make dry pot-pourri more attractive, whole, perfect flower heads can be dried in a desiccant such as borax, silica gel or sand:

BORAX: This is the lightest and best desiccant. Use either alone or mixed with an equal quantity of cornmeal.

SILICA GEL: Buy finely ground from the chemist or drug store. After use it must be re-dried: spread it out on a tray and dry it in a low oven until litmus paper turns blue when put to it.

SAND: This should be swished around in water to which a little detergent has been added and then drained and rinsed in several changes of water. After the final draining, spread it on trays and dry it for around three hours in the sun or in a warm oven.

Put a layer of the desiccant into a box which has an airtight lid, such as a plastic sandwich box. Dry one type of flower at a time. Make sure each has a short stem and push this gently into the desiccant. Using a small paint brush, work the desiccant around and between the petals, making sure that they are completely covered otherwise they may develop damp patches or become mildewed. Put in other flowers to complete the layer, leaving at least half an inch (1.5 cm) round each flower. Cover the flowers with a 1½ - 2 inch (4-5 cm) layer of desiccant.

Tape round the lid to keep it airtight, and leave the box in a dry, warm room. Small thin flowers, such as lily of the valley, will take about one day to dry; thick, fleshy ones, such as carnations and whole rose buds, will take up to four days. When you think drying is complete, test by gently removing the desiccant from one flower. It should be lightly crisp. When all the flowers are dry, shake off the desiccant using the paint brush again to make sure that it is all removed.

The flowers should look absolutely perfect and will have kept a good deal of their colour.

BASIC METHOD

1   Dry all the flowers and leaves so they are crisp.

2   Find a large container in which to mix the pot-pourri, such as an old glazed crock.

3   Put in the flowers and leaves.

4   Add spices, crushed citrus peels and fixative. Using your hands, mix well.

5   Add the oils, one drop at a time and mixing well after each addition.

6   Add whole citrus peel, whole spices and flowers for decoration. Mix again.

7   Put the pot-pourri into large jars or polythene bags and seal them tightly. Leave it for 6 weeks to mature, shaking every other day.

RECIPES

Here are some dry pot-pourri recipes to try. You don't have to stick to them exactly, as pot-pourri making always depends on availability of ingredients.

POT-POURRI OF GREEN HERBS

A lovely, refreshing mixture from the herb garden. Use it in the bedroom, living room, hall or nursery.

1 oz (25g) lemon verbena

1 oz (25g) orange blossom

2 oz (50g) lavender

½ oz (15g) lemon balm

2 oz (50g) rosemary

1 oz (25g) thyme

¼ oz (7.5g) bay leaves

½ oz (15g) lemon thyme

½ oz (15g) wormwood

1 oz (25g) peppermint

1 oz (25g) sage

1 oz (25g) cornflowers (or other blue flowers)

1 oz (25g) marigold flowers

1 tbsp crushed cardamom seeds

2 tbsp crushed cinnamon

1 oz (25g) crushed lemon peel

3 tbsp orris root powder

2 drops lavender oil

3 drops lemon oil

ROSE AND LAVENDER POT-POURRI

Sweet and slightly sharp for the living room or bedroom.

4 oz (100g) rose petals

2 oz (50g) lavender

1 oz (25g) lemon verbena

½ oz (15g) marjoram

½ oz (15g) rosemary

4 tbsp crushed orange peel

2 tbsp allspice berries, crushed

1 tbsp cloves, crushed

4 tbsp orris root powder

5 drops rose oil

3 drops lavender oil

FRESH GREEN POT-POURRI

Lovely for the kitchen and superb in any room for a cold in the head.

4 oz (100g) lavender

2 oz (50g) lemon verbena

2 oz (50g) southernwood

2 oz (50g) meadowsweet

2 oz (50g) peppermint

½ oz (15g) mint-scented geranium leaves

2 tsp nutmeg chips, crushed (these are what is left after you have grated most of the nutmeg. If not available, use ½ nutmeg, freshly grated)

2 tbsp crushed cinnamon

2 tbsp crushed lemon peel

4 tbsp gum benzoin

3 drops peppermint oil

5 drops lemon verbena oil

3 - 4 oz (75 - 100g) blue flowers for colour (optional)

SWEET ROSE POT-POURRI

Soft and delicate for bedroom or nursery.

4 oz (100g) rose petals

1 oz (25g) orange flowers

1 oz (25g) marjoram

16 bay leaves, crumbled

4 tbsp lavender flowers

4 tbsp lemon verbena

6 tbsp dried blue flowers for colour

2 tbsp crushed cinnamon

2 tbsp crushed cloves

2 tbsp bayberry powder

1 tbsp crushed orange peel

2 tbsp orris root powder

18 drops rose oil

3 drops orange blossom oil

DUSKY ROSE POT-POURRI

An aphrodisiac pot-pourri for the bedroom.

4 oz (100g) rose petals

2 oz (50g) jasmine flowers

1 oz (25g) orange flowers

2 oz (50g) sanderswood

1 oz (25g) sandalwood chips

4 tbsp cardamom seeds, crushed

2 tbsp crushed orange peel

4 tbsp orris root powder

5 drops musk oil

2 drops cypress oil

HERBY ROSE POT-POURRI

Fresh and sweet for the living room.

4 oz (100g) rose petals.

2 oz (50g) marjoram

1 oz (25g) bay leaves, crumbled

1 oz (25g) thyme

1 oz (25g) southernwood

1 oz (25g) hyssop

1 oz (25g) basil

2 oz (50g) blue flowers

1 oz (25g) hibiscus flowers (optional)

2 tbsp allspice berries, crushed

2 tsp coriander seeds, crushed

4 tbsp orris root powder

5 drops rose oil

3 drops magnolia oil

WOODY POT-POURRI

A mottled brown and yellow pot-pourri, good in the kitchen to keep away the flies.

1 ½ oz (40g) hyssop

1 oz (25g) southernwood

1 oz (25g) wormwood

1 oz (25g) tansy

½ oz (15g) marigold flowers

½ oz (15g) yellow everlasting flowers

1 tbsp sandalwood powder

1 ½ tsp crushed nutmeg chips

2 drops cypress oil

2 drops cedarwood oil

2 drops ylang ylang oil

2 tbsp gum benzoin

COTTAGE GARDEN POT-POURRI

This is an all-in-together pot-pourri made from flowers and leaves collected throughout the summer. It has a light, sweet scent and is suitable for any room.

3 oz (75g) lavender flowers

4 oz (100g) rose petals

1 oz (25g) peony petals

1 oz (25g) jasmine flowers

1 oz (25g) camomile flowers

1 oz (25g) carnation flowers

1 oz (25g) lemon balm

½ oz (15g) bay leaves, crushed

1 oz (25g) marjoram

1 oz (25g) hyssop

½ oz (15g) thyme

½ oz (15g) peppermint

1 oz (25g) southernwood

1 oz (25g) marigold flowers

1 oz (25g) meadowsweet

1 oz (25g) rosemary

1 oz (25g) everlasting flowers

1 oz (25g) dried blue flowers

4 tbsp crushed cinnamon

4 tbsp crushed allspice

4 tbsp crushed cloves

1 nutmeg, grated

2 oz (50g) crushed orange peel

2 oz (50g) orris root powder

2 drops each rose, honeysuckle, carnation, lilac and lavender oil

LEMON POT-POURRI

A refreshing pot-pourri for entrance hall or kitchen. It will also freshen the bedroom after the windows have been closed all winter.

1 oz (25g) lemon verbena

1 oz (25g) lemon balm

1 oz (25g) lemon thyme

½ oz (15g) marjoram

¼ oz (7.5g) bay leaves, crumbled

1 tbsp crushed lemon peel

6 tbsp crushed orange peel

2 tbsp orris root powder

2 drops orange blossom oil

2 drops lemon oil

RELAXING POT-POURRI

This is very soft and gentle, lovely in the nursery, bedroom or guest room.

2 oz (50g) rose petals.

1 oz (25g) camomile flowers

1 oz (25g) meadowsweet

1 oz (25g) agrimony

½ oz (15g) hibiscus flowers

½ oz (15g) lemon balm

8 bay leaves, crushed

1 tbsp crushed cinnamon

1 tbsp crushed vanilla pod

2 tsp crushed cloves

2 tsp crushed allspice

3 tbsp orris root powder

3 drops carnation oil

2 drops violet oil

ORIENTAL POT-POURRI

This has a dry, sweet scent. It can be used in the bedroom or sitting room.

2 oz (50g) rose petals

2 oz (50g) jasmine flowers

2 oz (50g) orange flowers

1 oz (25g) sweet basil

1 oz (25g) sanderswood chips

1 oz (25g) sandalwood chips

¼ oz (7.5g) ginger root, bruised and broken if possible.

2 tsp crushed anise seeds

2 tsp crushed coriander seeds

2 tsp crushed cumin seeds

3 tbsp gum benzoin powder

6 drops jasmine oil

MAKING A POT-POURRI
BY THE MOIST METHOD

A moist pot-pourri has a far stronger scent than a dry pot-pourri although the final result does not look so attractive. A moist pot-pourri should hold its fragrance for up to five years, and if well made, it could be used for up to fifty years.

Ingredients and method
Rose petals form the base of all moist pot-pourris which are made by 'curing' semi-dried petals and sweet-smelling flowers with salt in a crock. Later dried herbs, crushed or ground spices and fixatives are added and the mixture left to mature.

Using ½ pint (275 ml or 1 cup) of salt to every 1½ pints (850 ml or 3 cups) petals (measured tightly packed), arrange in layers, petals first, in a large crock to two-thirds full. Weight this down and leave the petals for two to six weeks, the longer the better.

If at first you do not have enough flowers you can fill the crock over several days (always stirring well before adding another layer) or, if it is large enough, all summer. After the last flowers have been added, leave for at least two weeks.

The mixture in the crock should dry out and cake, but if it starts to bubble and ferment, stir it every day but do not add any more flowers for at least a week. If excess moisture collects in the crock, you can carefully pour if off and add it to your bath water.

When all the petals have formed a dull, pink, dry cake, empty them onto a large, clean surface and break them up. Add 6 tablespoons dried herbs for every gallon of caked petals, plus no more than 10 oz (300g) mixed spices, fixatives and citrus peels, and store in an opaque container.

Put into a large China jar the following ingredients in layers, with bay salt strewed between the layers: two pecks [4 gallons] of damask roses, part in bud and part blown; violets, orange flowers and, with bay salt strewed between the layers: two pecks [4 gallons] of damask roses, part in bud and part blown; violets, orange flowers and jasmine, a handful of each; orris-root sliced, benjamin and storax, two ounces of each; a quarter of an ounce of musk; a quarter of a pound of angelica-root, sliced; two handsful of lavender flowers; half a handful of rosemary flowers; bay and laurel leaves, half a handful of each; three Seville oranges, stuck as full of cloves as possible, dried in a cool oven and pounded; half a handful of knotted marjoram; and two handsful of balm of Gilead dried. Cover all quite close. When the pot is uncovered, the perfume is very fine.

Domestic Cookery, 1834

RECIPES

Suggested mixtures for moist pot-pourri,
per gallon (4 litres) finished petals.

SWEET POT-POURRI

2 tbsp sweet marjoram

1 tbsp each thyme, bergamot.

crumbled bay leaves, lemon balm

dried crushed peel 1 orange

1 ½ oz (40g) orris root powder

1 oz (25g) gum benzoin

1 oz (25g) ground cloves

½ oz (15g) ground mace

½ oz (15g) ground allspice

½ oz (15g) powdered sandalwood

SWEET POT-POURRI WITH LAVENDER

6 tbsp dried lavender

2 tbsp sweet marjoram

1 tbsp rosemary

1 tbsp thyme

1 tbsp lemon balm

1 tbsp crumbled bay leaves

dried crushed peel 1 orange

3 oz (75g) orris root powder

½ (15g) ground cinnamon

½ oz (15g) ground cloves

½ oz (15g) ground nutmeg

LEMON POT-POURRI

2 tbsp lavender

2 tbsp lemon balm

2 tbsp lemon geranium

1 tbsp lemon verbena

1 tbsp southernwood

1 tbsp rosemary

dried crushed peel 1 lemon

1 ½ oz (40g) orris root powder

1 oz (25g) gum benzoin

½ oz (15g) ground mace

½ oz (15g) ground nutmeg

½ oz (15g) ground cinnamon

½ oz (15g) ground cloves

Mix the herbs and spice mixture into the petals by hand, making sure all the petals come into contact with the spices. The pot-pourri should smell very strong but 'raw'. Oils can be added very sparingly and gradually at this stage, but be careful. A matured moist pot-pourri should have a sweet enough scent of its own. It is best, therefore, to wait and add oils after the maturing process is complete.

To mature the pot-pourri, put it back into the crock, cover it tightly and leave it for 6 weeks, stirring every day.

A Sweet-smelling Perfume

Take a pound of fresh-gathered Orange flowers, of common Roses, Lavender Seeds, and Musk Roses, each half a pound; of Sweet Marjoram Leaves and Clove-July flowers picked, each a quarter of a pound; of Thyme, three ounces; of Myrtle Leaves, and Melilot Stalks stripped of their Leaves, each two ounces; of Rosemary Leaves, and Cloves bruised, each an ounce; of Bay Leaves, half an ounce.

Let these ingredients be mixed in a large pan covered with parchment, and be exposed to the heat of the sun during the whole summer; for the first month stirring them every other day with a stick, and taking them within doors in rainy weather. Towards the end of the season they will afford an excellent composition for a perfume; which may be rendered yet more fragrant, by adding a little scented Cypress-powder, mixed with coarse Violet-powder.

The Toilet of Flora, 1775

CONTAINERS FOR POT-POURRI

...you should hang your pot in an open chimney or near a continual fire so that the petals will keep exceeding fair in colour and be most delicate in scent

SIR HUGH PLATT,
Delights for Ladies, 1594

Traditionally, dry pot-pourris have been kept in open bowls so they can constantly add freshness and fragrance to a room. Moist pot-pourris have more frequently been kept in opaque, lidded containers which can be opened to release their fragrance only when the room is in use.

In the eighteenth and nineteenth centuries, elaborately decorated pot-pourri jars were a feature in many country houses and were examples of some of the finest porcelain of the period. They were patterned with birds and flowers and often had an outer, airtight lid which could be removed to reveal an inner, perforated one.

Dry pot-pourri today can still be kept in open bowls, but remember that its fragrance is transient and diminishes after a few weeks in the open. The bowls can be covered when the room is not in use, or the pot-pourri can be put into lidded glass jars and uncovered periodically.

Look out in antique shops for lidded sugar bowls or pretty serving dishes, open work silver caskets and unusual jars. Small, lidded baskets, with their tops decorated with dried flowers, also make good containers for a dry pot-pourri.

A traditional pot-pourri jar is still the best container for a moist pot-pourri. Porcelain ginger jars or any other lidded china jar will also be suitable. If a moist pot-pourri is to be kept in a glass container, either add plenty of coloured, dried flowers to it, or stick tiny dried flowers to the inside of the jar with a lightly beaten egg white before putting the pot-pourri inside.

Revitalising a pot-pourri
Both types of pot-pourri will last longer if they are kept away from damp and humid atmospheres.

If the scent starts to fade, add a few drops of an essential oil to a dry pot-pourri; add oil or brandy or eau-de-cologne to a moist one. You can also buy pot-pourri revivers.

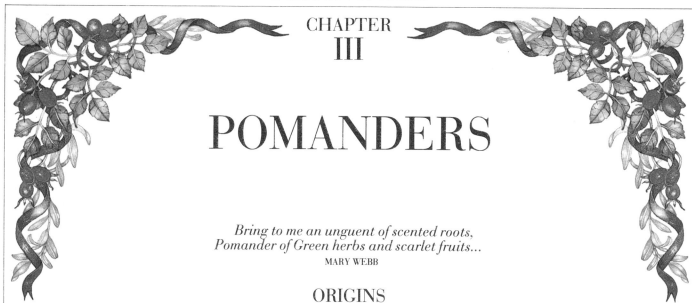

CHAPTER
III

POMANDERS

Bring to me an unguent of scented roots,
Pomander of Green herbs and scarlet fruits...
MARY WEBB

ORIGINS

References to pomanders can be traced back to the ancient Greeks, and later one is referred to in the medieval poem *Roman de la Rose*, in which it is called a 'pomme d'embre' or apple of amber. In those days, a pomander was a ball of musk, ambergris and other scented ingredients, about the size of a small apple, which was carried, worn or hung in chambers 'against foule, stinkying aire.' This type was used until the eighteenth century.

Henry V carried 'a musk ball of gold' which he obtained during his French campaign. In Tudor times, bracelets and necklaces made of small beads of perfumed gums were sold by tinkers. When they were worn, body temperature increased their scent and their believed effectiveness against disease.

In the court of Elizabeth I the spiced mixtures were worn in bejewelled gold and silver containers. The queen was given by a courtier 'a faire gyrdle of pomanders.' It was made in the form of six segments like those of an orange, grouped together round a central core and held in place by a ring. Each segment could be filled with a different perfume and opened separately. Deaths heads or flower shapes could also hold a pomander. Towards the end of the sixteenth century, similar spiced mixtures were put into a small box with a perforated lid known as a cassolette. Goa stones, a seventeenth century extravagance, included pounded precious jewels. A direct descendent of these original pomanders is the perforated pottery ball which we now hang in the bedroom or wardrobe.

MAKING A POMANDER
1 large orange
about 1 oz (25g) good quality cloves,
with strong stems and large heads
1 tbsp orris root powder
1 tbsp ground cinnamon

Gently knead the orange in your hands to soften the skin. Stick the cloves into the orange, leaving the width of one head all round each one. If the orange proves to be tough or the cloves too brittle, use a darning needle, bodkin or very fine knitting needle to pierce the outer skin, being very careful not to go right through. If a ribbon is to be tied round the finished pomander, leave a cross shape round the orange, the width of your chosen ribbon, free of cloves.

Mix together the orris root powder and cinnamon. Put them onto a sheet of greaseproof paper. Roll the orange in the mixture and pat it well in with your fingers. The orange should be quite coated with it. Wrap the orange in tissue paper and put it into a brown paper bag. Leave it in a dark, airy place to dry for two to three weeks.

Tie a ribbon round the orange, making a loop about six inches long to hang it by. Alternatively, if no cross was let for the ribbon, put the orange into a small, coloured net bag and thread ribbon through the top. An alternative mixture of cinnamon and cloves with the orris root may be used.

A Sweet and Delicate Pomander

Take two ounces of Labdanum, of Benjamin and Storax one ounce: musk, six grains; civet, six graines [six pinches]; Amber-grease, six graines; of *Calamus Aromaticus* and Lignum Aloes, of each the weight of a groat; beat all these in a hot mortar, and with a hot pestall till they come to a paste; then wet your hand with Rosewater and rowle up the paste suddenly.

SIR HUGH PLATT, *Delights for Ladies*, 1594

Spiced Rose Beads

1lb (450g) sweet-scented red rose petals

1 tsp ground cinnamon

1 tsp ground cloves

Put the rose petals into an enamel or stainless steel saucepan and barely cover them with water. Heat them gently, keeping them at below simmering point for 1 hour and taking care not to let them boil. Leave for 24 hours. Repeat this three times more, adding the cloves and cinnamon the last time the petals are heated.

You should now have a smooth paste. Wet your hands very lightly with rose water and roll small portions of mixture into small round beads against the palm of your hand. Put a hole through each one with a darning needle. Spread greaseproof paper over a cooling rack and lay the beads on it. Dry them in a sunny room or warm airing cupboard until hard.

Thread the beads onto thick thread and wear them round your neck like the original pomander. The warmer they become, the stronger will be their scent.

Orange and clove pomander

The orange stuck with cloves, which we have come to recognise as the pomander, was first used by Cardinal

Wolsey. He carried it when visiting his parishioners and held it near his nose to counteract the bad smells of the streets and to ward off disease. Since then, these pretty, sweet-smelling fruits have been hung in rooms and linen cupboards and laid amongst clothes and handkerchiefs in drawers.

Soak the cloves for a few hours in orange flower oil before using. In this case, drying will definitely take three weeks. The dried pomander can be painted with an essential oil such as carnation and then dried for a further week. For decoration, small dried whole flower heads can be stuck onto the ribbon or pinned onto the net bag.

Renewing the Scent of a Pomander

The scent of a pomander should last for many years. When it begins to fade it can be lightly painted with an aromatic oil to renew its life:

Take one grain [a pinch] of Civet, and two [2 pinches] of Musk, or if you double the Proportion it will be so much the sweeter: grinde them upon a stone with a little Rose-water, and after, wetting your hands with Rose water, you may worke the same in your Pomander. This is a sleight to pass away an old Pomander: but my intention is honest.

SIR HUGH PLATT, *Delights for Ladies*, 1594

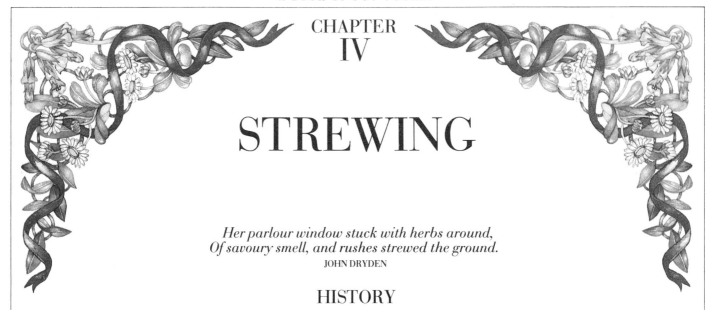

CHAPTER
IV

STREWING

Her parlour window stuck with herbs around,
Of savoury smell, and rushes strewed the ground.
JOHN DRYDEN

HISTORY

Strewing, the covering of floors with sweet-scented plants, was a custom brought to Britain by the Romans. They scattered flowers on the floors of banqueting halls and in front of processions, and bay leaves covered the floors of the houses of high-ranking officials.

In Saxon, Norman and Tudor England, floors were strewn not only to provide a pleasing scent; some plants used kept away fleas, others helped combat disease, and all provided a herbal 'carpet' which was pleasant to sit on: ' ...their chambers and parlours strewed over with sweet herbs, refreshed me' said a visitor to sixteenth-century England.

Besides manor houses and halls, church floors were also strewn, very often with sweet rushes, and, until the end of the seventeenth century, flowers were strewn over the pews. Herbs were always strewn in front of the monarch at coronations, even as late as the coronation of George IV: 'Miss Fellowes with her six tributary herb-women heading the grand procession, appeared at the gate of the Abbey.'

My lady's fair pew has been strewn full gay
With primroses, cowslips and violets sweet
With mints, with marigolds, and marjorams.

C. seventeenth century

STREWING HERBS OF ALL SORTS

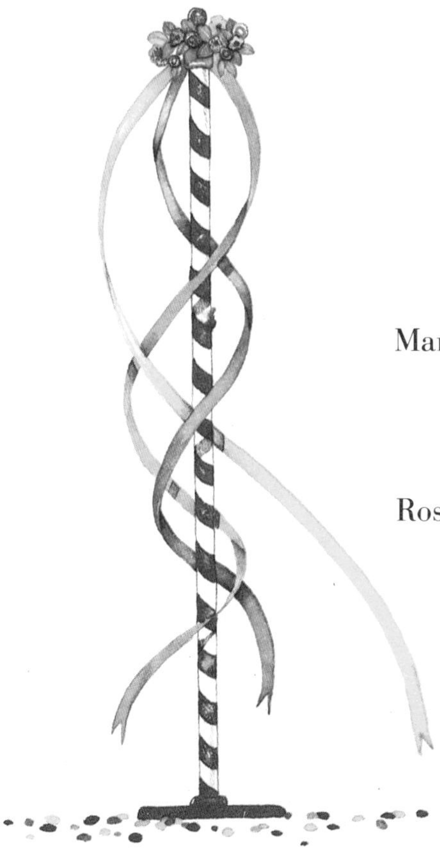

Bassell, fine and busht, sowe in May

Bawlme, set in Marche

Camamel

Costemary

Cowsleps and paggles

Daisies of all sorts

Sweet fennel

Germander

Hop, set in Februarie

Lavender

Lavender spike

Lavender cotten

Marjorom, knotted, sow or set, at the spring

Mawdelin

Peny ryall

Roses of all sorts, in January and September

Red myntes

Sage

Tansey

Violets

Winter savery

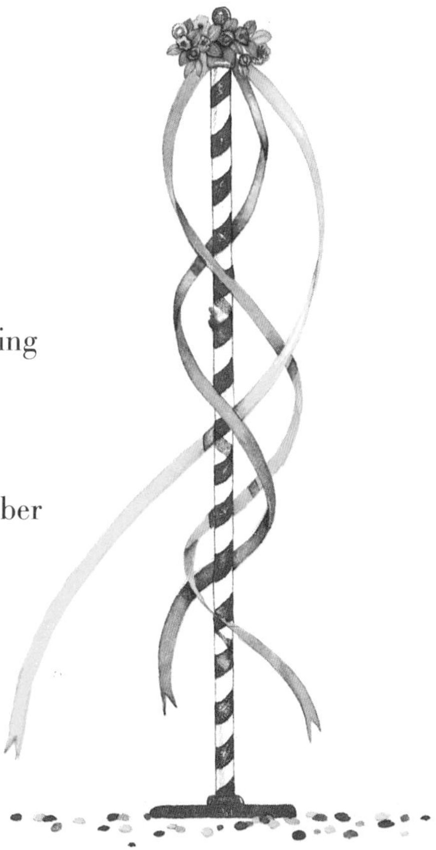

THOMAS TUSSER, 1573

Herbs used for strewing include:

SWEET FLAG (ACORUS CALAMUS) : A favourite for many years, both in churches and cathedrals, and in the houses of the wealthy. It grew only in the fen country and so was much used in Norwich and Ely Cathedrals. Some was also imported from Europe. Sweet flag was expensive, and Cardinal Wolsey was reprimanded by the king for being too extravagant with it at Hampton Court. The only drawback with sweet flag was that it attracted insects, so fleabane had to be burned in the room whenever it was replaced with fresh plants.

MEADOWSWEET: Elizabeth I's favourite. Its leaves 'far excell all other strewing herbs to deck up houses, to strew chambers, halls and banqueting houses in summer time, for the smell thereof makes the heart merry and joyful and delighteth the sense.' GERARD

GERMANDER: Much used for its soft, sweet scent.

HYSSOP: 'Pretty and sweet.' Parkinson, 1640.

LEMON BALM: Scent only released when walked on.

BAY: Fresh leaves used by the Elizabethans.

BASIL: Releases sharp, refreshing scent when stepped upon.

TANSY: Drives away fleas and flies; fresh, camphor smell.

WORMWOOD: Kept away insects.

JUNIPER: A pine-like, healthy smell.

MYRTLE: A distinct, but slightly antiseptic aroma.

> While wormwood hath seed, get a bundle or twain,
> to save against March, to make flea to refrain:
> Where chamber is sweept, and wormwood is strown,
> no flea, for his life, dare abide to be known.
>
> THOMAS TUSSER, 1573

Strewing Herbs Today

Today, strewing fresh or dried herbs over carpets would hardly be practical. However, if you have rush matting that is permanently down in one room, try sprinkling it with dried, sweet-smelling herbs such as a mixture of lavender and roseroot, crumbled bay leaves, lavender, meadowsweet, rosemary, roseroot, or woodruff.

And let the ground whereas her foot shall tread,
For feare the stones her tender foot should wrong,
Be strewed with fragrant flowers all along,
And diapered like the discoloured mead.

EDMUND SPENSER, seventeenth century

CHAPTER
V

PERFUMING ROOMS

On the table...stands a little saucer with precious,
sweet-smelling Geranium leaves.
MRS EARLE, *Pot-Pourri from a Surrey Garden*, 1905

SWEETENING THE AIR

The simplest way of perfuming a room is of course to place in it pots or vases of sweet-scented flowers.

Bunches of aromatic herbs hung up in summer will have a cooling effect on the air, and some will keep away flies. Lavender and rosemary have long been used for this purpose, and the whole plant of roseroot will keep the air sweet for a long time. Wormwood keeps the air cool and deters flies, and woodruff brings a scent of new-mown hay.

Hanged up in houses, it doth very well attemper the aire, coole and make fresh the place to the delight and comfort of such as are therein.

JOHN GERARD, 1597

Herbs to deter flies: Basil, Camomile, Hemp agrimony, Mugwort, Pennyroyal, Peppermint, Rue, Tansy.

Herbs to sweeten the air: Bay, Cotton lavender, Germander, Hyssop, Lavender, Lemon balm, Mint, Rosemary, Thyme, Woodruff, Wormwood.

Lavender can be used in the following ways to deter flies:

1   Add a few drops of oil of lavender to a jug of boiling water and place in the room.

2   Moisten a sponge with boiling water. Put on a few drops of oil of lavender and keep the sponge in a dish in the room. Moisten the sponge with boiling water twice a day and add a few more drops of oil twice a week.

MAKING FLOWER AND HERB SACKS

Dry pot-pourri mixtures or simpler mixtures of dried, sweet-smelling flowers and herbs can be sewn into silk or cotton bags or sachets and hung round the room or on the backs of chairs.

In the kitchen, make small hessian bags and fill them with sharper herb mixtures which will combat cooking smells and keep away flies. Squeeze them as you walk past to release their scent.

RECIPES

LEMON KITCHEN MIXTURE

3 oz (75g) lemon verbena

1 oz (25g) lemon geranium leaves

1 oz (25g) peppermint

2 pieces dried lemon peel, crushed

2 tbsp orris root powder

Mix all the ingredients together well.

MRS EARLE'S SACHET

2 oz (50g) lavender flowers

1 oz (25g) lemon verbena leaves

1 oz (25g) lemon- or mint-scented geranium leaves

1 tbsp orris root powder

Put the lavender, lemon verbena and geranium leaves into a bowl and mix in the orris root powder with your hands, making sure it comes into contact with all the ingredients. To increase the perfume two drops of oil of lavender can be added if wished.

FRESH KITCHEN MIXTURE

2 oz (50g) lemon verbena

1 oz (25g) bay leaves, crumbled

1 oz (25g) spearmint, or mixed mints

½ oz (15g) lovage

2 tsp cloves, crushed

1 ½ tbsp orris root powder

Mix all the ingredients together well.

On the backs of my armchairs are thin Liberty silk oblong bags, like miniature saddle-bags, filled with dried Lavender, Sweet Verbena, and Sweet Geranium leaves. This mixture is much more fragrant than the lavender alone. The visitor who leans back in his chair wonders from where the scent comes.

MRS EARLE, *Pot-pourri from a Surrey Garden*, 1905

CHAPTER
VI

BURNING PERFUMES

*...be sure every morning to perfume the house with angelica
seeds, burnt in a fire-pan or chafing dish of coales.*
STEVENSON, 1661

The word perfume comes from the Latin 'per' meaning
through, and 'fumare' to smoke. The custom of burning
aromatics has now been forgotten but for many centuries it
was thought to be the best method of perfuming rooms,
purifying the air and keeping away infection. Most houses
and inns owned perfuming pans and where they did not,
herbs were simply burnt on an open fire. Some perfume
recipes used only rose water, sugar and spices, others were
more complicated, using gum benzoin and other aromatics
which were made into small cakes similar to incense.

A Very Good Perfume to Burn

Take two ounces of the Powder of Juniper Wood, one
Ounce of Benjamin, one ounce of Storax, six drops of
oil of lemons, as much oil of Cloves, ten grains [10
pinches] of Musk, six [6 pinches] of Civet, mould them
up with a little gum-Dragon steeped in Rosewater,
make them in little Cakes and dry them between Rose
leaves, yoiur Juniper Wood must be well dried, beaten
and searced.

The Queen's Closet Opened, 1662

If you have an open fire, you can easily perfume a room by putting herb trimmings onto the embers. Try lavender, bay and angelica seeds.

In the seventeenth century students at Oxford burnt juniper wood 'to sweeten their chambers'. The dried roots of elecampane will give a musty scent. Rosemary on a fire is relaxing, and southernwood will refresh at the end of a tiring day.

Herb mixtures such as rosemary and lavender; rosemary, southernwood and thyme; lavender and mint; lavender and sage, can be burned in metal incense burners.

Lavender Incense

Remove the flowers from dried lavender. Soak the stems in salt petre water as above for 30 minutes. Dry them completely. Stick the ends into either a ball of plasticine or a jar of dry sand. Light them and they will burn slowly like incense.

To Remove Unpleasant Smells

Cut brown paper into 4 inch (10cm) squares. Dissolve 1 tablespoon salt petre in ½ pint (275 ml) 1 cup warm water. Soak the paper in the water for 10 minutes and then dry it completely. Put one piece of paper into an old tin plate or dish. Sprinkle on 2 tablespoons dried lavender flowers. Set light to them.

The French Queen's Perfume

First burn chips of Cypress in the Chamber a pretty
while, the doors and windows being shut. Then take
Damask Rose water a pint: white Sugar Candy an
ounce: Put them in a perfuming pan and let them boyl
softly on the embers.

WILLIAM SALMON, *Polygraphics* seventeenth century

CHAPTER
VII

PERFUMING LINENS

*Let's go to that house, for the linen looks white and smells of
lavender and I long to be in a pair of sheets that smell so.*
IZAAK WALTON

HERBS FOR SCENTING LINEN

'Lavender' comes from the Latin 'Lavare', to wash. The
lady who once washed the clothes and hung them on
lavender and rosemary bushes to dry was called a
'lavenderess'. Once dry, the clothes were folded with
lavender sprigs amongst them and put away in sweetly-
scented chests.

Scenting linens and clothes with fragrant herbs made
them pleasant to use and wear, masked the smells of the
sometimes unwashed people who used them, and also kept
away moths and fleas.

Herbs suitable to lay among linen include:

LAVENDER: A clean scent that deters moths and will protect
clothes 'from dirty, filthy beasts'. Lay sprigs in drawers and
chests or hang them in the airing cupboard. 'Pure lavender,
to lay in a bridal gown.' (Leigh-Hunt)

LAVENDER STICKS: These you can make: just before the flowers
open, cut them with the longest stalks possible. Trim all the
stalks to the same length. Separate them into bundles of

And still she slept an
azure-lidded sleep,
In blanched linen, smooth
and lavender'd

JOHN KEATS,
The Eve of St. Agnes

twenty and tie each bundle with strong thread, just under the flower heads. Do not tie the thread so tight that it cuts into the stalks. Bend the stalks back over the flower heads, spacing them evenly to make a 'basket'. Tie the stalks again as close to the flower heads as possible. Hang the bunches up to dry in a warm, airy place, away from direct heat or sunlight. Tie ribbon over the last thread tie. This can be laid in drawers or hung in wardrobes or on coathangers by a ribbon loop.

ROSEMARY: 'Also take the flowres and put them in a chest amonge your clothes or amonge bookes and moughtes [moths] shall not hurte them.' (BANKES' HERBAL, 1525)

FEVERFEW: Keeps away all types of insects.

HYSSOP: This has a clean, fresh scent.

THYME: Suitable for laying amongst furs and winter clothes.

COTTON LAVENDER: This is probably the best moth deterrant. Tie it in sprays with rosemary or lavender.

TANSY: Keeps away fleas and lice.

WOODRUFF: This has a sweet, hay-like scent to deter moths.

MUGWORT: This may take its name from the Saxon 'moughte' for moth.

SOUTHERNWOOD: A hay-scented moth deterrent.

COSTMARY: This gives a balsam-like scent: '...to lye upon the toppes of beds, presses, etc., for the sweet scent and savour it casteth.' (PARKINSON, 1640)

WORMWOOD: '...this herb Wormwood being laid among cloaths will make a moth scorn to meddle with the cloaths as much as a lion scorns to meddle with a mouse or an eagle with a fly.' (CULPEPPER, 1652).

SWEET BAGS

Small sachets of dried herbs and petals have been used in the linen cupboard for centuries. They provide more complex scents than sprigs of herbs, as spices and fixatives can be added to the mixtures. They also prevent pieces of scratchy herbs finding their way into beds. Lavender has such a strong, definite, long-lasting scent that it can be used alone in sweet bags. Lavender bags are traditionally made from lavender-coloured organdie or voile, tied with lavender ribbon.

To scent drawers you can put several drops of essential oil on a piece of cotton wool and rub it well into the inside of a wooden drawer. Alternatively, buy a roll of cheap wallpaper (the cheaper the better as it is more absorbent). Measure out the length that you will need for all the drawers together. Unroll it and scatter it thickly with a dry pot-pourri or sweet bag mixture and roll it up again. Seal it in a polythene bag and leave it for six weeks, by which time it should have absorbed the perfume. Cut it into lengths and use it as a drawer liner.

It was once a custom to rinse linens and clothes after they were washed in sweet-scented waters, usually rose or lavender. Special scents were also kept in what were called 'casting bottles' to be sprinkled over linen before they were folded or put away:

Sweet-scented powders were also scattered over clothes and linens before they were put away.

BASIC RECIPE

Dry all the petals and herbs until they are crisp, as for a dry pot-pourri. Finely crumble them, but do not reduce them to powder.

Natural fibres, such as cotton and silk, are best for sweet bags. They enable the herbs to breathe and release their perfumes. The exceptions are coloured nylon net, which

must be used double, and man-made muslins and organdies on which you can embroider flower patterns. Sweet bags can be any size or shape depending on the amount of herbs and material you have available. Make them square, oblong, hexagonal, triangular, round or heart-shaped. Use pretty ginghams, floral prints or broderie anglaise and edge them with gathered ribbons or lace.

Do not fill sweet bags too full. Make them fairly loosely packed and the herb mixtures will release their fragrance more easily. As a rough guide, a 2 ounce (50g) mixture will fill an oblong bag that is 6 by 8 inches (15x20 cm).

VICTORIAN SWEET BAG

1 oz (25g) thyme

1 oz (25g) rosemary

½ oz (15g) cloves, crushed

2 tsp orris root powder

ELIZABETHAN SWEET BAG

1 oz (25g) rose petals

1 oz (25g) lavender flowers

2 tbsp clove pink petals

½ oz marjoram

1 tbsp cloves, crushed

1 tbsp orris root powder

SWEET BAG FOR MEN

2 oz (50g) lemon verbena

1 oz (25g) peppermint

dried rind 1 lemon, crushed

1 tbsp cloves, crushed

1 tbsp orris root powder

MOTH DETERRING BAG

1 oz (25g) cotton lavender

1 oz (25g) lavender flowers

½ oz (15g) rosemary

1 tbsp orris root powder

CLEAN SCENTED BAGS

1 oz (25g) lavender flowers

1 oz (25g) hyssop

½ oz (15g) lemon verbena

1 tsp ground nutmeg

1 tbsp orris root powder

ROSE OR LAVENDER SCENTED LINEN

Add ½ pint (275 ml or 1 cup) rose water or ¼ pint (150 ml or ½ cup) lavender water to 1 gallon (4 litres) rinsing water. Sprinkle rose or lavender water over sheets before ironing them.

CHAPTER
VIII

SWEET SLEEP

There sleeps Titania sometime of the night,
Lulled in these flowers with dances and delight.
SHAKESPEARE, *A Midsummer Night's Dream*

SLEEP PILLOWS

For many centuries, both mattresses and pillows have been stuffed with scented grasses. The Romans were the first to add dried rose petals to pillows, and Elizabethan mattresses were often stuffed with Lady's Bedstrew (*Galium odorata*). George III could not sleep without his hop pillow, and Victorian ladies favoured lavender, turning their faces towards the sweet scent and inhaling it to calm their fluttering hearts.

Sleep pillows delicately perfume the bedroom and help to relax and to calm jangled nerves. They sweeten the sick room, help the elderly, and calm fractious babies. They are a perfect pleasure to have around.

I judge that the flowers of lavender quilted in a cap and worne are good for all diseases of the head that come from a cold cause and that they comfort the braine very well.

WILLIAM TURNER, *New Herball*, 1551

HERBS FOR SWEET SLEEP

HOPS: Dried hops smell sweet and have a pleasantly narcotic effect. They are also very soft and so suitable for stuffing a large pillow. You can mix woodruff, agrimony and southernwood with hops; all are sweetly-scented and help to induce sleep. Bay and rosemary can be added for a sharper scent. Lemon verbena and mint give a clean scent, as does lemon balm but it is more soothing. Lavender does not go well with hops.

LAVENDER: This is good in the sick room, and very refreshing. It can be mixed with rose petals.

MARJORAM: Mix with woodruff, agrimony and southernwood.

ROSEMARY: 'Put the leaves under thy bedde and thou shalt be delivered of all evil dreames.' (BANKES' *Herbal*, 1525)

SPICES: Cloves help to clear the head and can prevent snoring. Cinnamon, allspice, lemon and orange peels, orris root and pine needles can also be added.

OTHER HERBS: These should be used in mixtures – Clover, Cowslip, Mignonette, Peppermint, Lime flowers, Camomile, Sage, Catmint, Bergamot, Thyme, Angelica, Valerian. Valerian is very bitter, so use it sparingly.

The leves layde under the heade whanne a man sleeps, it doth away evell spirites and suffereth not to dreame fow le dremed ne to be afeade.

THE COUNTESS OF HAINAULT,
fourteenth century

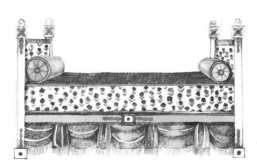

51

MAKING SLEEP PILLOWS

A pillow made mainly from hops can be made the size of a normal pillow since it will be soft enough for you to rest your head on. Other herbs which are harder and more scratchy are best made into sachets measuring about 10 by 8 inches (25 x 20 cm). These are put inside the pillow ticking, or can be placed under the pillow or hung by a ribbon from the headboard and placed under your cheek when you need to inhale the strong scent of the flowers.

For a full-sized pillow you will need 1lb (450g) of hop mixture. For a 10 by 8 inches (30x20cm) you will need 2-2 ½ ounces (50-65g) of hop or any other herbal mixture. If a sachet is to be placed permanently inside the pillow ticking, it need only be made from a plain material and left undecorated. Use white muslin or even larger white handkerchiefs.

Sachets for hanging on the headboard or laying under or on a pillow should have an inner cover of muslin and an outer cover of a pretty, washable material, hand sewn at one end for easy removal. Choose pretty cottons and silks to match the decor of the bedroom and edge them with lace or ribbon.

If you feel that the scents of your pillows are not strong enough, 1-3 drops of essential oil may be added, one drop at a time and mixing well after each addition.

Lavender pillows help to clear head colds. You can also wear a small lavender sachet in a mop cap at night, or make a cap with lavender flowers:

We made no end of sleepy-pillows; every one of our beds had one, a large linen bag filled with a proper quantity of hops and dried cowslips, dried in their season.

ELIZABETH YANDELL, c.1900

HERB PILLOW MIXTURES

These can be increased or decreased in proportion to suit the size of the pillow you are making. Crush the herbs slightly before mixing

FRESH LAVENDER PILLOW

1 oz (25g) lavender flowers

4 bay leaves, crumbled

½ oz (15g) lemon thyme

½ oz (15g) sweet marjoram

2 tbsp rosemary

1 tbsp crushed cinnamon

1 tbsp orris root powder

COUNTRY PILLOW

1 oz (25g) woodruff

½ oz (15g) agrimony

½ oz (15g) southernwood

3 bay leaves, crumbled

2 tbsp rosemary

1 tbsp orris root powder

HOP PILLOW

8 oz (225g) hops

2 oz (50g) woodruff

2 oz (50g) agrimony

2 oz (50g) southernwood

ROSEMARY AND LEMON PILLOW

1 oz (25g) rosemary

1 oz (25g) lemon verbena

2 tbsp peppermint

1 tbsp crushed, dried lemon peel

1 tbsp orris root powder

LAVENDER AND ROSE PILLOW

1 oz (25g) lavender flowers

1 oz (25g) rose petals

½ oz (15g) lemon verbena

1 tbsp rosemary

2 tsp cloves, crushed

1 tbsp orris root powder

Pillows for the Sleepless, 1700

Of strong linen, close woven. A strip fifteen inches wide and thirty six deep. Fold to make a bag eighteen inches deep. Seam and fell all sides, leaving a space on one end to admit the stuffing.

Take of cowslips and fresh hops, newly dried, as many as you deem enough to make a soft cushion in equal parts. Distribute your hops and cowslips nicely, in a bowl, and proceed to stuff your pillow until you feel it comfortable to the head. Over-sew the opening and your pillow is made.

Those who by reason of great grief, study or long watchfulness cannot catch their sleep will find such a pillow serviceable.

CHAPTER
IX

PERFUMED CLEANLINESS

It is also well to boil the flowers and leaves in water
and to wash yourself therewith every morning...
THE PHYSICIANS OF MYDDRAI, seventeenth century

SWEET WASHING WATERS

Rose water was first made in tenth-century Persia, and since Norman times this and other delicately scented floral waters were much favoured by English ladies, both for washing the hands at table and for cleansing the face and body in bedroom and bathroom.

In the days before proper cutlery came into use, bowls of scented water were always placed on the tables of manor house and castle. They were often made of silver, ornately worked and bejewelled. The washing bowl given to Queen Matilda by Geoffrey of Anjou was shaped like a peacock. In Tudor times sweet waters were kept in 'casting bottles' for the table and used not only to wash the hands, but were sprinkled over the table, the food and the clothes of the diners.

Washing with sweet waters, especially those distilled from fragrant flowers and rain or spring water, has always been believed to beautify the complexion. Waters made from rose petals, lavender, rosemary, marjoram, pennyroyal and basil were once kept in elegant ewers in the bedroom.

Take a gallon of faire water, one handfull of Lavender flowers, a few Cloves and some Orace powder and foure ounces of Benjamin; distill the water in an ordinary leaden Still. You may distill a second Water by a new infusion of water upon the leaves; a little of this will sweeten a bason of faire water for your table.

SIR HUGH PLATT,
Delights for Ladies, 1594

Finger Bowls for the Dinner Table

All through the summer a slight surprise and pleasure
comes at the end of a little dinner if a buttonhole of
sweet-smelling flowers and leaves are carefully tied up
(fine wire does them the least clumsily) and dropped
into the water in the finger-bowls. Nothing should be
used but what is really sweet – Lemon-scented
Verbena and Geranium leaves being the principal
foundation; and in summer there ought always to be
plenty of these two in the smallest gardens.

MRS EARLE, 1905

MAKING ROSE WATER

Some do put rose water in a glass and they cut roses
with their dew thereto and they make it to boile in
water then thei set it in the sune tyll it be readde and
this water is beste.

ASKHAM'S *Herbal,* 1550

Making rose water by distilling
Put 1lb (450g) fresh, sweet-scented red or pink rose petals
or 12 oz (350g) dried red rose petals into a large kettle. Half
fill the kettle with rain or spring water. Attach a rubber tube
to the spout. Set the kettle on a low heat. Run the tube
through a basin of ice-cold water and let it hang into a jug or
bottle. Let the water in the kettle simmer until it has all
evaporated and the jug or bottle contains pure rose water.
Throughout the process, frequently replace the iced water or
top up the bowl with ice cubes.

Making rose water in the oven
Put 2lb (900g) fresh, sweet-scented, red or pink rose petals
or 1 ¼lb (575g) dried rose petals into a large earthenware,
enamel or stainless steel casserole. Cover them with rain
water or spring water. Heat the oven (450°F, 220°C, gas
mark 6). Put in the casserole and bring the water to boiling
point. Cover and leave the casserole in the oven for a further
15 minutes. Cool the water and strain it.

Easy rose water

Put 1 oz (25g) fresh or ½ oz (15g) dried, sweet-scented red or pink rose petals into a basin. Pour on ½ pint (275ml or 1 cup) boiling water. Cover and leave for 1 hour. Strain and bottle. Although this is convenient, it does not have as strong a scent as rose waters made by other methods.

The cheat's rose water

Mix together 4 pints (2.15 litres or 8 cups) distilled water and 1 tablespoon essence of roses. Bottle, shake well and leave for a week before using.

Roseroot water

This was often used as a cheaper substitute for rose water. Wash and chop 2lb (900g) roots of roseroot. Put them into a saucepan with 1 pint (575 ml or 2 cups) spring water or rain water. Bring them to simmering point, cover and simmer for 1 hour. Cool, covered, and strain.

Rosemary water

Put 4 tablespoons chopped rosemary tips into a saucepan with ¾ pint (425 ml or 1 ½ cups) water. Bring them to simmering point, cover and simmer for 30 minutes. Cool, strain and bottle. Rosemary water can also be made by distilling as for rose water.

Lavender, marjoram, pennyroyal and basil waters may be made either by distilling, or as given for rosemary water.

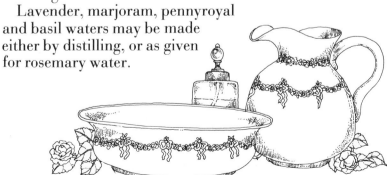

HERBAL BATHS

Lying back in an aromatic bath is one of the greatest of pleasures. According to the herbs that you use, it can relax and calm you, revive you and stimulate you into action, ease aching limbs, or help a tired circulation. So fill the bath with hot, but not too hot, water, put in a non-slip mat, spoil yourself by putting a pillow under your head, and have ready a large, warm, rough towel.

Herbs for the bath

ROSEMARY: Used by the Romans to relieve tired limbs after a long march; relieves stiff joints and relaxes aching muscles

PEPPERMINT and LEMON BALM: Mix with rosemary or use alone

MEADOWSWEET: A refreshing smell; eases tired limbs

HYSSOP: Good for stiffness after overwork or sport

LAVENDER: Clean, refreshing scent; natural disinfectant

BLACKBERRY LEAVES: Very invigorating

PLANTAIN LEAVES: Use for skin ailments

BAY LEAVES: Comfort aching limbs

PENNYROYAL: Refreshing scent 'to comfort the nerves'

LOVAGE: A natural deodorant: 'This herbe for hys swete savoure is used in bathe' (Thomas Hyll, 1577)

CAMOMILE: Very soothing and relaxing

ELDER LEAVES and FLOWERS: Healing and stimulating

LEMON BALM: Very relaxing

LIME FLOWERS: Very calming

BORAGE, SAGE, TANSY: Enlivening

MUGWORT: Relieves tiredness and makes limbs supple

VALERIAN: Very soothing, but it has a bitter scent

If thou hast wisdom,
hear me, Celia,
Thy baths shall be the
juice of July-flowers,
Spirit of Roses,
and of Violets,
The milk of unicorns, and
panther's breath
Gathered in bags and
mixed with Cretan wines

BEN JONSON,
Volpone

To Make a Bath for Melancholy

Take Mallowes, pellitory of the wall, of each three handfulls; Camomell flowers, Melilot flowers, of each one handfull; hollyhocks, two handfulls; Isop, one great handfull, senerick seed one ounce, and boil them in nine gallons of Water untill they come to three, then put in a quart of new milke and go into it bloud warm or something warmer.

Arcana Fairfaxiana, circa seventeenth century

Suggested mixtures:

PEPPERMINT, ROSEMARY, LEMON BALM

ROSEMARY, SAGE, MINT

LEMON BALM, ROSE GERANIUM, LAVENDER

LAVENDER, ROSEMARY, CAMOMILE

LAVENDER, THYME

ROSE, LAVENDER, THYME

LIME, LEMON BALM, VALERIAN (TINY AMOUNT)

Using herbs in the bath

Do not put fresh or dried herbs directly into the bath water. They will stick to your skin, round the edges of the bath and round the plug hole. The best way is to make a strong infusion or decoction of the herbs and add it to the bath while the taps are still running.

For an infusion, put 1 oz (25g) fresh herbs or ½ oz (15g) dried into a jug. Pour on 1 pint (575 ml or 2 cups) boiling water. Cover and leave until cool. Strain.

For a decoction, simmer 6 tablespoons chopped, fresh herbs or 3 tablespoons dried in 1 pint (575 ml or 2 cups) water, covered, for 30 minutes. Take from the heat and leave covered until cool. Strain.

A Sweet Scented Bath

Take of Roses, Citron peel, Sweet flowers, Orange flowers, Jessamy, Bays, Rosemary, Lavender, Mint, Pennyroyal, of each a sufficient quantity, boil them together gently and make a Bath to which add Oyl of Spike six drops, musk five grains, Ambergris three grains.

The Receipt Book of John Middleton, 1734

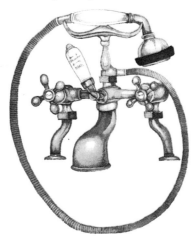

Washing bags

Another way of obtaining the scent of herbs for the bath is to put them into small muslin bags. These can then be hung so that the water from the taps runs through them before entering the bath. A bag containing 4 tablespoons dried herbs will release enough perfume and it can be used two or three times, depending on the quality of the herbs.

Oatmeal bags

Oatmeal is a well-known skin softener. Make bags containing 2 tablespoons medium oatmeal and 2 tablespoons dried herbs. Use them like the herb bags.

Soapy bags

Make slightly larger bags. Mix together 2 tablespoons medium oatmeal, 2 tablespoons dried herbs and 1 tablespoon grated, unscented soap. Use like the herb bags.

Cornmeal washing bag

Make the bag thin and flat. Fill it with a mixture of equal parts of cornmeal and dried herbs. Use this as a washing mitt. The cornmeal will cleanse the skin and remove any dead cells.

Herbal bath vinegar

Cider vinegar added to the bath will soften the skin. To make a herbal bath vinegar, put 3 tablespoons dried herbs into a jug. Heat together ½ pint (275 ml or 1 cup) each cider vinegar and water to just below boiling point. Pour them over the herbs. Cover and leave for 12 hours. Strain. Add ½ pint (275 ml or 1 cup) to the bath water while the taps are running.

Bath oils

Ideally, a fragrant bath oil should be one that will disperse readily in the water. If it does not disperse it will float on the top and only coat your skin as you get out.

The only oil which will disperse well is treated castor oil, known as turkey red oil. Mix this with essential oils of flowers and herbs. You will need 3 tablespoons turkey red oil to 1 tablespoon essential oil. Put them into a bottle and shake them well. Add 1 teaspoon only to each bath.

If turkey red oil is not available, use a non-dispersing, odourless oil such as almond, avocado, sunflower or untreated castor oil. Use the same proportions and again add only 1 teaspoon to each bath.

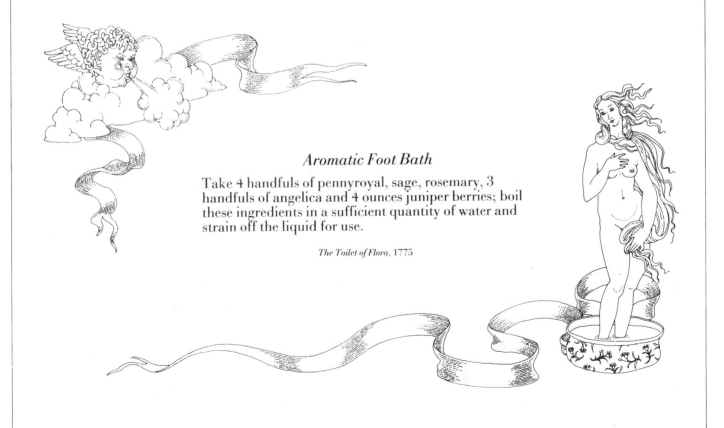

Aromatic Foot Bath

Take 4 handfuls of pennyroyal, sage, rosemary, 3 handfuls of angelica and 4 ounces juniper berries; boil these ingredients in a sufficient quantity of water and strain off the liquid for use.

The Toilet of Flora, 1775

PERFUMED SOAP AND WASHBALLS

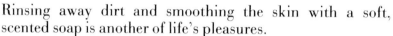

Take a quarter of a pound of *Calamus Aromaticus*, a quarter of a pound of Lavender flowers, six ounces of Orris, two ounces of Rose leaves, and an ounce of Cypress; pound all these together in a Mortar and rub them through a fine sieve, then scrape Castile soap, and dissolve it in Rose-Water, put in your beaten Powder, pownd it in a Mortar, and make it up into Balls.

The Receipt Book of John Nott, Cook to the Duke of Bolton, 1723

Rinsing away dirt and smoothing the skin with a soft, scented soap is another of life's pleasures.

Soap was not really popular until the Victorian era. Before this it was mostly imported, expensive and taxed highly. In very early times most people could not obtain any kind of soap. Instead the herb soapwort (*Sapponaria officinalis*) was used which 'scoureth almost as well as soap' (Gerard, 1597). The Anglo-Saxons mixed it with willow ash and simmered it in rain water. Medieval monks called it Fuller's Earth and another name for it was Bouncing Bet.

The Normans and Tudors cared little for baths, preferring to mask body odours with strong perfumes. Even Elizabeth I only bathed once a month, but when she did she used herbal infusions and perfumed washballs. Washballs were made from a rich, white soap called Castile soap which was imported from Spain. Mixed with it were all kinds of herbs, spices, fixatives and barks to make coarse-textured, rather grainy coloured balls which acted rather like a loofah on the skin, besides cleansing it. These were used until the end of the eighteenth century.

To the Victorians cleanliness was important and they insisted on a daily bath. As a result, the home manufacture of ordinary soap was greatly increased and perfected, and the previous high taxes were lifted.

RECIPES

SCENTED SOAP

Soak some cotton wool or gauze in lavender, rose or another flower oil. Wrap it round several bars of unscented soap. Seal in a polythene bag and leave for two months.

BATH SOAP

4 tsp caustic soda	
½ pint water	
2 tbsp almond oil	
2 tbsp coconut oil	
2 tbsp glycerine	
2 tsp honey	
2-3 drops flower oil	

Put the water into a large pyrex bowl. Wearing rubber gloves, stir in the caustic soda with a wooden spoon and keep stirring until it has dissolved. Put the oils, glycerine and honey into a saucepan and warm them on a low heat so they combine. Stir them immediately into the soda solution. Stir in the flower oil and keep stirring vigorously until the mixture becomes white and thick. If it should start to set, stand the bowl in warm water. Line small moulds with clingfilm. (yoghurt pots or egg poachers will be fine if nothing else is available). Pour in the mixture. Cover the tins with clingfilm and leave them in a warm, dry place for 24 hours for the soap to set. Use the clingfilm to lift the soap out of the moulds. Then peel it off and wrap the soap in greaseproof paper.

FLORAL WASHBALLS

Two 5 oz (150g) bars Castile soap	
½ pint (275 ml) 1 cup rose water, plus extra for polishing	
10 drops oil of cloves	
3 tbsp dried lavender flowers, crushed	
3 tbsp dried red rose petals, crushed	
2 tbsp dried sweet marjoram, crushed	

Flake the soap with a sharp knife or grate it. Put it into a large mixing bowl. Heat the rose water to just below boiling point and pour it over the soap. Stir with a wooden spoon. Leave for 10 minutes and then knead with

your hands to make a smooth, white paste. Mix in the oil of cloves, lavender, rose petals and marjoram. Leave the mixture for 10 minutes in a warm place until it has begun to dry and is mouldable. Form it into twelve small balls, about the size of a golf ball. Leave them in the sun or in a warm place on a baking sheet covered with clingfilm to firm for about 2 hours. They should not be completely dry. Moisten your hands with rose water and rub the balls until they become smooth and shiny. Put them back onto the clingfilm and leave them in a warm place for 24 hours to firm completely.

SOAPWORT WASHING LATHER

Put 1 ½ oz (40g) soapwort leaves or roots or a mixture into 1 pint (575 ml) 2 cups rain or spring water in a saucepan. Gradually bring them to the boil and boil for 4 minutes. Cool, covered, and strain, pressing down the leaves. Store in a screw-topped bottle. Use ¼ pint (150 ml) ½ cup in the bath.

OATMEAL SOAP

As the recipe for bath soap, but add 2 tablespoons of medium oatmeal with the flower oil.

TALCUM POWDERS

Talcum powders first became fashionable in Elizabethan times. Besides being used on the body, they were rubbed on clothes and gloves. The queen had a special powder made up for her from orris root, dried rose petals, calamus and ground cloves.

You may take of Rose leaves four ounces, cloves one ounce, lignum Rhodium two ounces, Storax one ounce and a halfe, Muske and Civet of each ten grains [10 pinches]; beat and incorporate them well together.

RAM'S *Little Dadoen*, 1606

Making Talcum Powder

The base for a talcum powder can be made of one or more of the following: unscented talcum powder, cornflour, rice flour or precipitated chalk. Add essential oil, herbal infusions or floral waters for scent and fix the scent with orris root powder.

Boric acid powder will give slight antiseptic properties.

Take 2lbs [900g] of orris root, ground to a powder; 2 ozs [50g] of sweet marjoram; 2 ozs of calamus root; ½lb of sieved rose petals, which have been dried; ½ drachm [1/16 oz or 1 ½g] of cloves and of musk. Pound together until the whole has become a sweet scented powder which retains perfume for a year or more.

— PHILIPPE GUIBERT, Physician Regent in Paris, early seventeenth century

BASIC MIXTURE

3 oz (75g) unscented talcum powder or precipitated chalk

3 oz (75g) rice flour or cornflour

½ tbsp boric acid powder, or crystals, crushed

1 tbsp orris root powder

1 tsp essential oil

Mix the dry ingredients. Add the oil and rub it in with your fingertips until it is absorbed and the mixture feels dry. Sieve twice. Pack the powder into a box and apply it with a large dusting puff. To add scent to your powder you will need: 1 teaspoon of herbal infusion or floral water per 2 oz (50g) dry mixture. Mix them in with your fingertips until the powder feels dry. Extra can be added if the scent is not strong enough, but take care not to get the mixture too wet. Sieve twice once dry.

CHAPTER
X

FRAGRANT BEAUTY

But flowers distilled, though they with winter meet,
Lose but thir show, their substance still lives sweet.
SHAKESPEARE

SWEET WATERS FOR THE COMPLEXION

Flowers and herbs can be made into many preparations, for cleansing, toning and beautifying the skin.

Sweet waters for the complexion are easy to make by distilling as for rose water or by making infusions or decoctions. Make an infusion by steeping 1 oz (25g) fresh herbs or ½ oz (15g) dried, covered, in 1 pint (575 ml or 2 cups) boiling water until cold. For a decoction, simmer the herbs in the water for 15 minutes, covered. Cool and strain.

Herbs and flowers that can be used include:

ROSE: Soothes the skin after exposure to strong winds or sun. It softens chapped skin and makes a refreshing bath for the eyes.

ROSE WATER AND WITCH HAZEL ASTRINGENT: Shake together 6 tablespoons of rose water and 2 tablespoons of witch hazel.

ROSEROOT: This soothes a wearied face and smooths out wrinkles produced by tiredness.

ELDER FLOWERS: This is a mild astringent which tones the skin. It is particularly good applied after using a greasy cleanser. If the sea air has made your face sore, gently warm ¼ pint (150 ml or ½ cup) elder flower water, and dissolve in it ½ a teaspoon of borax and 2 tablespoons of glycerine. Cool and apply to the face.

ELDER FLOWER TONER: Put 1 oz (25g) dried elder flowers into a jug. Pour on 1 oz (575 ml or 2 cups) boiling water, cover and cool slightly. Add 1 tablespoon vodka. Cover and keep in a warm place for 4 hours. Cool, strain and bottle.

CAMOMILE: Regular bathing will help to reduce wrinkles. It is slightly antiseptic and benefits an oily skin. It is particularly effective when mixed with rosemary.

ROSEMARY: This was the important ingredient in Hungary Water, which was said to have preserved the beauty of Queen Elizabeth of Hungary so well that she was proposed to by the king of Poland when she was in her seventies.

Mix together 4 fl oz (125 ml or ½ cup) rose water and 4 tablespoons witch hazel or vodka. Add 2 tablespoons each chopped rosemary and mint. Cover and leave for 48 hours, stirring frequently. Strain, pressing down well on the herbs and bottle. Nearly every old manuscript has a different recipe, but the rosemary is always there:

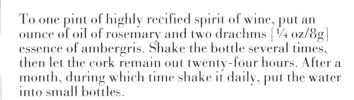

To one pint of highly recified spirit of wine, put an ounce of oil of rosemary and two drachms [¼ oz/8g] essence of ambergris. Shake the bottle several times, then let the cork remain out twenty-four hours. After a month, during which time shake it daily, put the water into small bottles.

The Receipt Book of Susannah Stacy, nineteenth century

YARROW: Also good for an oily skin; a light astringent.

WOODRUFF: This freshens the complexion and is soothing after exposure to sun or wind.

SAGE: Sage is an invigorating and cleansing astringent. To make sage water: 'Take sage flowers, sprinkle them with white wine or water. Let them stand awhile. Then distil them.' (*The Receipt Book of Joseph Cooper*, 1654)

LEMON BALM: This helps to smooth wrinkles. One of the main ingredients of Carmelite Water which was first made by the nuns of the Abbey of St Just in 1379. *The London Dispensary* of 1696 said that it would 'cure baldness and renew youth.'

LIME FLOWERS, CHERVIL: Both help to smooth wrinkles.

NETTLE: Cleansing and toning, nettle gives a pleasant tingle to the face.

LADY'S MANTLE: This is a mild astringent which was used by the ancient Arabs.

MYRTLE: This is said to have been used by Venus.

A Curious Water of Mirtle Flowers

The flowers and leaves of mirtle, two handfuls, infuse them in two quarts of spring water, and a quart of white wine, twenty-four hours, and then distil them in a cold still and this will be of a strong scent and tincture, and by adding more or less of the mirtle you may make it stronger or weaker as you please. This beautifies, and mixed with cordial syrups is a good cordial and inclines those that drink it to be very amorous.

STEAM CLEANSING THE FACE

...the large red cabbage-rose lent its colour and perfume to a pink-scented ointment. This was much favoured by the ladies of the household when they went to balls, and gave a glorious tint to the complexion besides a sweet fragrance.

MARCUS WOODWARD *The Mistress of Stanton's Farm*, 1938

Holding the face over fragrant steam will cleanse the pores and help to tighten the skin. It is not, however, to be recommended for those with sensitive skin or broken veins.

To make the steamer, put 2 tablespoons fresh herbs or 1 tablespoon dried into a jug. Pour on 1 pint (575 ml or 2 cups) boiling water. Hold your face 12 inches (35 cm) away from the water and cover your head with a towel. Steam for 15 minutes. Wipe the moisture from your face with cotton wool and then close the pores by splashing with a herbal astringent.

Use the following herbs according to your needs:

CAMOMILE with THYME or LAVENDER: Cleansing and soothing

ROSEMARY, NETTLE: To boost the circulation and to cleanse

YARROW, SAGE: Astringents

PEPPERMINT, ELDER FLOWER: Skin tightening

COMFREY, FENNEL: To heal

FENNEL, NETTLE, LIME: To remove impurities

REMOVING FRECKLES AND LIGHTENING THE SKIN

To Take Away Freckles in the Face

Wash your face, in the wane of the Moone, with a sponge, morning and evening, with the distilled water of Elder-leaves, letting the same dry into the skinne. Your water must be distilled in May. This from a Traveller, who hat cured himself thereby.

SIR HUGH PLATT, *Delights for Ladies*, 1659

To have any effect herbal infusions and decoctions to remove freckles should be used regularly over a long period.

Elizabeth I used elder flower water mixed with lemon juice. Use 3 tablespoons elder flower water, 1 tablespoon lemon juice and a pinch of alum.

Other herbs that can be used include:

PARSLEY: Make an infusion with 2 oz (50g) freshly chopped parsley and ½ pint (275 ml) boiling water. Use night and morning as facewash.

DANDELION: Make an infusion with 1 oz (25g) chopped fresh leaves and ½ pint (275 ml) boiling water. Use night and morning as facewash.

TANSY: Soak the leaves in buttermilk for ten days, 'when it should make the complexion very fair.' (COLES, *The Art of Simpling*).

ROSEMARY: 'Boyle the leaves in white wine and washe thy face therewith and they browes and thou shalt have a faire face.'

The roots of the madonna lily were once boiled in water until the water was reduced to one third. The decoction was applied to the face on nine successive nights.

LOTIONS AND CLEANSERS

I have heard that if maids will take wild Tansy and lay it to soak in Buttermilk for the space of nine days and wash their faces therewith, it will make them look very faire.

The Virtuose Boke of Distyllation, Master Jerom Brunswyke, 1527

ELDER FLOWER CLEANSING MILK

¼ pint (150 ml) buttermilk

2 tbsp dried elder blossoms

1 tbsp honey

Put the elder flowers and buttermilk into a saucepan and gently bring them to just below simmering point. Keep them there for 30 minutes. Remove from the heat and stir in the honey. Leave for three hours and strain. This should be used within 1 week and ideally should be kept in a cold place or in the refrigerator.

ROSE WATER MOISTURE LOTION

4 tbsp glycerine

3 tbsp rose water

Pour the glycerine and rose water into a bottle and shake them well together.

ROSEMARY ASTRINGENT LOTION

3 tbsp strong rosemary infusion, warm

¼ tsp borax

3 tbsp rose water

2 tsp witch hazel

Put the infusion into a bowl. Sprinkle in the borax and stir for it to dissolve. Cool. Stir in the rose water and witch hazel. Bottle and shake.

LIME FLOWER CLEANSING MILK

Make as for the elder flower cleansing milk, but substituting lime flowers.

FOR A FACE WASH

Take a quart of wild strawberries, wild tansy, three pintes of new Milke. Still as these together and wash your face therein.

The Good Housewife's Handmaid, 1585

CREAMS

To Make Oyntment of Roses

Take oyl of Roses four ounces, white wax one ounce, melt them together over seething water, then chafe them together with Rose-water and a little white vinegar.

JOHN PARTRIDGE,
The Treasurie of Hidden Secrets and Commodious Conceipts, 1586

COLD CREAM

½ oz (15g) beeswax

3 fl oz (90 ml or 3/8 cup) almond oil

4 tbsp distilled water or rose water

¼ tsp borax

1 drop oil of rose

Put the wax and oil into a double saucepan and melt them over a low heat. Warm the distilled water or rose water, put in the borax and swirl it round until it has completely dissolved. Beat the solution into the wax and oil. Add the rose oil. Take the pan from the heat and beat vigorously (either with a wooden spoon or electric beater) until the mixture is cool and creamy textured. Pour it into clean pots. Cool completely before covering.

Galen invented cold cream and the recipe now is very much the same as it was two thousand years ago. In the sixteenth century it was prepared with oil of cole-seed, which produced the name. Then it was spread on cloth and worn as a face mask at night.

HERBAL COLD CREAM

Use the recipe for cold cream, but replace the rose water with a herbal infusion such as rosemary, elder flower, lemon balm or woodruff. Herbal oil or oil of lemon can be added instead of the rose oil.

MARIGOLD FACE CREAM

4 fl oz (125 ml ½ cup) almond oil

2 tbsp lanolin

petals from 6 marigold flowers

Put the almond oil and lanolin into a double boiler. Add the marigold petals and keep at just below simmering point for 30 minutes. Strain quickly into a small pot. Use after exposure to the sun.

HONEY AND LANOLIN CLEANSING CREAM

½ oz (15g) beeswax

1 oz (25g) lanolin

3 fl oz (90 ml or 3/8 cup) almond oil of avocado oil

2 tbsp rose water or herbal infusion, such as elder flower, rosemary or sage

2 tsp honey

2 drops flower or herb oil

Put the wax and lanolin into a double boiler and melt them gently over a low heat. Remove the pan from the heat, but keep the top standing in the water. Using a wooden spoon, slowly add the almond oil. Stir in the rose water and honey. Add the flower oil. Pour the mixture into clean pots. Cool it completely before covering.

TO SOFTEN THE HANDS AND SOOTHE CHAPPED LIPS

Paste for Chapped Hands

Mix a quarter of a pound of unsalted hog's lard, which has been washed in water and then rose water, with the yolks of two new laid eggs, and a large spoonful of honey. Add as much fine oatmeal, or almond paste, as will work it into a paste.

The Receipt Book of Susannah Stacey, nineteenth century

ELDER FLOWER HAND CREAM

6 oz (160g) petroleum jelly

½ oz (15g) beeswax

4 oz (100g) fresh elder flowers or 2 oz (50g) dried

Put the petroleum jelly and beeswax into a small casserole and melt them together on a low heat, without letting them boil. Stir in the elder flowers. Cover and put in a preheated oven (200°F, 100°C, gas mark under ¼) for 4 hours. Strain through muslin or a nylon sieve directly into a pot. Let the cream cool and firm before covering.

MARY DOGGETT'S LIP SALVE

4 tbsp olive oil

½ oz (15g) beeswax

2 tbsp chopped rosemary

2 tbsp rose water

Put the oil and beeswax into a double saucepan and melt them gently on a low heat. Stir in the rosemary and the rose water. Keep at just below simmering point for 30 minutes. Strain quickly into a pot. Cool completely before covering.

A REFRESHING HANDWASH AFTER GARDENING

4 fl oz (125 ml or ½ cup) elder flower water

1 tbsp glycerine

HONEY LIP SALVE

4 tbsp honey

1 tsp lavender, rose or elder flower water

Put the honey into a small pan. Bring it to just below boiling point and skim it. Remove it from the heat, pour it into a bowl and stir in the floral water. Pot. Rub it on the lips before going to sleep.

ROSE WATER HAND SOFTENER

2 tbsp cornflower

4 fl oz (125 ml or ½ cup) rose water

2 tbsp glycerine

juice ½ lemon

In a bowl, mix the cornflour with 4 tablespoons of the rose water. Put the remaining rose water into a saucepan with the glycerine and heat them gently. Stir in the cornflour mixture and lemon juice and simmer, stirring, until the mixture is thick. Take it from the heat and put it into a pot. Cool and cover.

FOR BRIGHT, LIVELY EYES

To soothe tired eyes or help bloodshot eyes, bath with a tepid, mild infusion of any of these herbs: elder flower, eyebright, camomile, coltsfoot, fennel or parsley.

To brighten and strengthen the eyes
Simmer 2 tablespoons fresh or 1 tablespoon dried eyebright in ½ pint (275 ml or 1 cup) milk for 15 minutes. Cool completely. Soak pads of lint or cotton wool in the milk. Lay down with the pads over your eyes for at least 15 minutes.

To reduce puffiness round the eyes
Soak pads of lint or cotton wool in infusions of rosehip tea, or lemon verbena infusion (2 tablespoons dried to ½ pint [275 ml or 1 cup] boiling water), or elder flower infusion (2 tablespoons dried to ½ pint [275 ml or 1 cup] boiling water) All these infusions must be used cold. Lay the pads over your eyes and lie down for at least 15 minutes.

TO CLEAN THE TEETH AND SWEETEN THE BREATH

Method of Making the Teeth Beautifully White

Take dried leaves of hyssop, wild thyme, and mint, of each half an ounce, of roach alum, prepared hartshorn, and salt, of each a dram [1/8 oz or 3g]; calcine the ingredients together in a pot placed on burning coals; when sufficiently calcined, add thereto pepper and mastic, of each half a dram; myrrh, a scruple [1g]; reduce the whole to a very fine powder, and mix into the consistency of an opiate with storax dissolved in rose-water. Rub the teeth with a small bit of this opiate every morning and afterwards wash the mouth with warm wine.

The Receipt Book of Susannah Stacey, nineteenth century

SAGE TOOTH POWDER

1 oz (25g) fresh red sage leaves

1 oz (25g) coarse sea salt (Maldon is best)

Mix the sage and salt together. Spread them on a baking tray. Put them in a preheated oven (300°F, 150°C, gas mark 2) for 20 minutes, or until the sage is crisp and dry. Pound the mixture with a pestle and mortar and then sieve it. Use with a soft brush instead of toothpaste.

For sweet breath

Rosemary tea was once recommended to be drunk by butlers before they served at banquets. It would sweeten their breath so they would not offend those they were serving. Simmer ½ oz (15g) fresh rosemary tops in 1 pint (575 ml or 2 cups) water for 10 minutes. Strain and drink one wine glass full three times a day.

Peppermint tea, made as an infusion, will also cleanse the system and sweeten the breath. Use 1 tablespoon fresh or 2 teaspoons dried to ½ pint (275 ml or 1 cup) water.

To counteract the smell of garlic, eat parsley or watercress.

To clean the teeth

Sage is the most effective herb for the teeth. The fresh leaves of red sage, rubbed over the teeth, will whiten them, freshen the breath and strengthen the gums.

SAGE AND PEPPERMINT TOOTH POWDER

Use method for sage tooth powder substituting ½ oz (12g) red sage and ½ oz (12g) peppermint leaves.

HERBS FOR BEAUTIFUL HAIR

To Preserve Hair and Make it Grow Thick

Take one queart of white wine, put in one handful of rosemary flowers, half a pound of honey, distill together; then add a quarter of a pint of oil of sweet almonds, shake it very well together, put a little of it into a cup, warm it blood warm, rub it well in your head and comb it dry.

HANNAH GLASSE, *The Art of Cookery Made Plain and Easy*, 1769

HERBAL SHAMPOO

4 tbsp fresh chopped herbs or 2 tbsp dried

¼ pint (150 ml or ½ cup) spring water or rain water

8 fl oz (225 ml or 1 cup) baby shampoo

Use rosemary as a general hair tonic, camomile for blonde or light brown hair and sage for dark hair. Simmer the herb in the water for 15 minutes. Strain and cool. Mix it with the shampoo. Bottle.

Hair rinses

The best tonic rinse is made with rosemary. It gives lustre, stimulates the scalp and makes the hair easier to set. Simmer 1 oz (25g) fresh or ½ oz (15g) dried rosemary in 1 pint (575 ml or 2 cups) water for 15 minutes. Cool and strain. Pour it over the hair several times if possible.

Other herbs for rinsing include:

VERVAIN: Infusion of the tops of vervain mixed with rosemary promotes growth and gives lustre

CAMOMILE: Brings out the colour of blonde

YARROW mixed with CAMOMILE: Good for light hair

RED SAGE: Makes dark hair shine

SOUTHERNWOOD: 1 teaspoon boiled with 2 tablespoons quassia chips in 1 pint (575 ml or 2 cups) water for 15 minutes and cooled gives lustre to dark hair. Nettles, lime flowers, fennel or elder flowers can be added to any other herbal rinse.

ROSEMARY DRY SHAMPOO

½ oz (15g) fuller's earth

4 drops oil of rosemary

Mix the fuller's earth and oil by pounding them together with a large pestle and mortar. Sieve. To use, sprinkle the powder into the hair and work it well in with your hands. Leave it for 10 minutes before brushing out with a soft bristle brush.

To prevent dandruff

An infusion of thyme and rosemary, used as a rinse and massaged in well is an effective remedy. Use a rosemary infusion with 1 teaspoon borax added to every ½ pint (275 ml or 1 cup) and massage it into the scalp daily.

To prevent falling hair and to promote hair growth

Infuse ½ oz (15g) southernwood in 1 pint (575 ml or 2 cups) boiling water until cold. Strain. Massage into the scalp night and morning. This is more effective if the southernwood is mixed with rosemary. You can also make several pints of the infusion and use it, hot, to dampen several tea towels. Wrap them round your head and leave them for 5 minutes.

An infusion of yarrow and rosemary massaged daily into the scalp will also promote hair growth and give lustre, and massaging a few drops each of oil of wormwood and oil of rosemary into the hair daily is also beneficial.

Southernwood was once known as Lad's Love as it was said to promote the grown of a new beard. 'The ashes thereof, mingled with old sallet oyl, halps those what have their hair fallen and are bald causing the hair to grow again, either on the head or on the beard.'

CULPEPPER, 1652 -

CHAPTER
XI

SCENTS AND PERFUMES

So you have a most grateful and odiferous water.

Perfumes have long been used both to mask body odours and to increase attractiveness.

Elizabeth I made perfumery fashionable in England and most country houses had their own still. Courtiers carried their perfumes in small chastened silver bottles which were hung from the shoulder or waist. The commercial distillation of lavender began in the early seventeenth century and lavender water became the favourite perfume of Nell Gwynne.

In the eighteenth century, a shop in London called The Sign of the Old Civet Cat was famous for its perfumes, one of which was used by George IV at state balls.

Perfumes can be made by distilling, by steeping herbs and flowers in alcohol, or by mixing alcohol with essential oils.

Eau Sans Pareil

One quart of spirits of wine, one ounce of essence of bergamot, two drachms [¼ oz or 6g] of tincture of musk, add to them half a pint of water, and bottle them for use.

HANNAH GLASSE, *The Art of Cookery Made Plain and Easy*, 1769

COLOGNES

To Make Sweet Water

Take Damaske Roses at discretion, Basil, Sweet Marjoram, Lavender, Walnut Leafs, of each two handfuls, Rosemary one handful, a little Balm, Cloves, Cinnamon one ounce, Bayleaf, Rosemary tops, Limon and Orange Pills of each a few; Pour upon these as much white wine as will conveniently wet them, and let them infuse ten or twelve days; then distill it off.

SIR KENELM DIGBY, *Receipts in Physick and Chirurgery*, 1668

COOKIE'S TOILET WATER, 1723

Spirits of wine 2 pints

Essence of violets 1 ounce

Spirits of rosemary 1 ounce

Essence of bergamot 1 drachm [1/8 oz or 3g]

Oil of verbena 1 drachm

Essence of jasmine 1 drachm

Orange flower water 1 ounce

Rosewater ½ pint

Mix and filter through blotting paper. Bottle for the toilet.

ROSE AND LAVENDER COLOGNE

¼ pint (150 ml or ½ cup) fresh, sweet-scented rose petals

¼ pint (150 ml or ½ cup) fresh lavender flowers

¼ pint (150 ml or ½ cup) 70% proof alcohol

2 tbsp thinly pared lemon peel

2 tbsp thinly pared orange peel

¼ pint (150 ml or ½ cup) boiling water

Put the rose petals and alcohol into a jar. Cover them tightly and leave them for 6 days. The day before they are ready, put the lemon and orange peels and lavender flowers into a jug. Pour in the boiling water, cover and leave overnight. Strain the alcohol from the rose petals, pressing down well, and mix with the lavender infusion. Put the mixture into a bottle and shake it well. Leave for 1 week before using, shaking every day.

FLORAL VINEGARS

Floral vinegars have been used for centuries both as beauty treatments and to ward off infections in the sick room. Sponges soaked in vinegar were carried in the tip of a doctor's cane in the seventeenth and eighteenth centuries, and Victorian ladies revived themselves with vinegar-filled smelling bottles and dabbed vinegar or their brows and temples when they were feeling 'indisposed'.

Flowers to use for vinegar include: basil, clove pink, dill, scented geranium leaves, honeysuckle, jasmine, lavender, lemon verbena, mignonette, rose, rosemary and violet.

Uses of floral vinegar

Floral vinegars have a far more refreshing scent than floral waters made with alcohol. They are therefore good in the sick room, lavender being the most effective. Soak a small sponge in the vinegar and leave it in a dish near the bedside.

To relieve headaches, use vinegars for a soothing compress, either neat or mixed with an equal quantity of spring water.

After exposure to the hot sun, dab a floral vinegar behind the ears and on the temples and forehead.

Vinegar will also soften both facial and body skin.

Roses: Do make a very pleasant and comfortable vinegar, good to be used in time of contagious sickness, and very profitable at all times, for such as have feeble spirits.

JOHN EVELYN, 1699

Clove pink: This is a most excellent and refreshing liquor to smell at by those afflicted with headache. It is also good to sprinkle the room of sick persons.

Herbal Delights
MRS C F LEYEL, 1937.

FLORAL VINEGAR

Fresh flower petals or herbs ¾ pint [425 ml or 1½ cups]

White wine or cider vinegar 1 pint [575 ml or 2 cups]

Put flower petals or herbs into a large bottle. Gently warm wine or cider vinegar, then pour over petals or herbs. Leave bottle on sunny window sill for 2 weeks. Strain. Repeat if scent not strong enough. To clear dry, mottled skin and as a general tonic, add ½ pint [275 ml or 1 cup] floral vinegar to the bath.

ASTRINGENT LOTION FOR OILY SKIN

Floral vinegar 1 tablespoon

Distilled water ¼ pint [150 ml or ½ cup]

Mix and bottle. Apply to face. Do not use soap first as vinegar decomposes soap residue.

FACE WASH

Lavender vinegar 2 tablespoons

Rose water 8 fl oz [225 ml or 1 cup]

Mix and bottle and apply directly to face.

To Make Vinegar of Roses

In summer time when roses blowe, gather them, ere they be full spred or blowne out, and in drie weather, pluck the leaves, let them lie half a day upon a faire borde, then have a vessel with vinegar of one or two gallons (if you will make so much Roses), put therein a great quantity of ye said leaves, stop the vesell close after you have styrred them wel together, let it stand a day and a night, then divide your Vinegar and Rose leaves together into two parts, put them in two great glasses, set them upon a shelfe under a wall side, on the south side without your house, where the sunne may come to them the most part of the day, let them stand there all the whole summer long; and then strain the Vinegar from the Roses and keep the Vinegar. If you do once in ten days take and straine out the Rose leaves and put in new leaves of half a dayes gathering the Vinegar will have more favour and odour of the Rose.

JOHN PARTRIDGE,
The Treasurie of Hidden Secrets and Commodious Conceipts, 1586

CHAPTER
XII

ESSENTIAL OILS

*This is a pleasant perfume, and being mixt with oils
and ointments, gives them a gratefull smell.*
JOHN FREUD, *The Art of Distillation*, 1652

Floral and herbal oils have many uses. They were once necessary for anointing and embalming, and have played a part in religious rites. They can be used in the making of toilet waters and scents, soaps, creams and pot-pourris. Add them to the bath or use them for massage.

The 'life force' of a plant is contained in its essential oil. Small amounts only can be extracted, but a little goes a long way. The most effective way of obtaining the oil is by distillation, and most commercial oils have been produced in this way, making them stronger than any that you can produce yourself. Others may have been expressed or extracted in other ways, producing a wide variation in quality.

The story goes that attar of roses, the essential oil of the rose, was first discovered by the Emperor Jehangir, one of the Mogul rulers of India. When he married, he had all the canals filled with rose petals. When walking beside them with his bride, they noticed an oily film appearing on the surface of the water, apparently produced by the action of the sun. It smelt like concentrated rose petals and so the

To Enable One To See The Fairies

A pint of sallet oyle and put it into a vial glasse: and first wash it with rose-water and marigolde water; the flowers to be gathered towards the east. Wash it till the oyle becomes white, then put it into the glasse, and then put thereto the budds of hollyhocke, the flowers of marygolde, the flowers or toppes of wilde thyme, the budds of young hazel and the thyme must be gathered near the side of a hill where the fairies used to be; and take the grasse of a fairy throne, then all these put into the oyle in the glasse and sette it to dissolve three dayes in the sun, and then keep it for thy use.

Emperor ordered it to be bottled, and thus it became one of the most precious scents of the royal household.

Although the distillation of herbs for oil was started in the sixth century, the most common and certainly the easiest way of extracting it was by macerating the petals in good quality oil.

To make attar of roses
Collect sweetly-scented rose petals put them into a large earthenware jar and cover them with distilled water. Place net or muslin over the top to keep out any insects and stand the jar in hot sun every day. When a thin film of oil appears on the surface, gently lift it off with cotton wool and squeeze it into a small glass bottle. Cover it tightly. Continue every day until no more oil appears.

Oils to use
Good quality, odourless oils such as olive, safflower, almond or sesame are best. Suitable flowers include rose, jasmine, lilac, violet, orange blossom, tuberose, lavender and honeysuckle. The best herbs to use are lemon balm, lemon verbena, rosemary, sage and peppermint.

Method for making essential oils
If using fresh flowers or leaves, bruise them, fill a glass jar, and cover with oil. Stand the jar in the hot sun for 48 hours. Strain, pressing down well. Repeat up to ten times to obtain the strength of oil required.

If using dried flowers or leaves, allow 3 tablespoons per ½ pint (275 ml or 1 cup) oil. Crush them and put them into a 1 pint (575 ml) bottle, pour in the oil and leave them in the sun for 3 weeks, stand the bottle in a saucepan of water and gently warm it on a low heat, without boiling the water, for two hours each day. Strain the oil, pressing down well. If the scent is not strong enough, repeat the process.

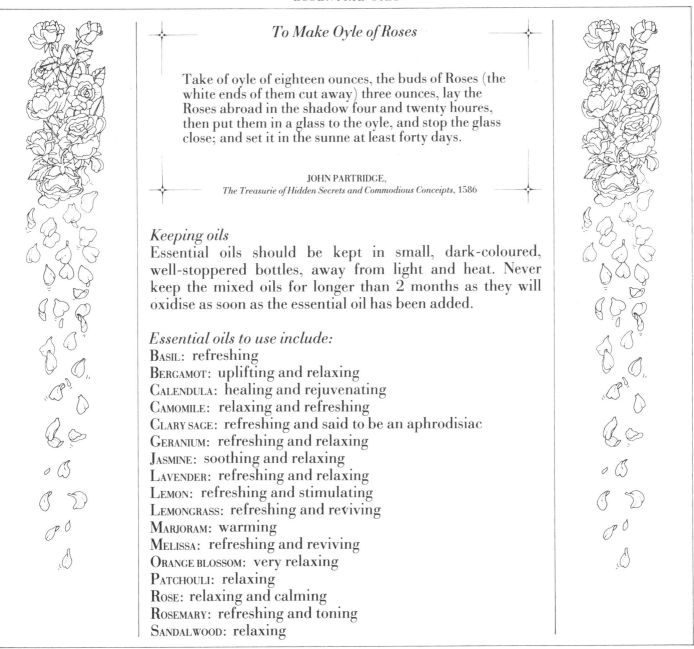

To Make Oyle of Roses

Take of oyle of eighteen ounces, the buds of Roses (the white ends of them cut away) three ounces, lay the Roses abroad in the shadow four and twenty houres, then put them in a glass to the oyle, and stop the glass close; and set it in the sunne at least forty days.

JOHN PARTRIDGE,
The Treasurie of Hidden Secrets and Commodious Conceipts, 1586

Keeping oils
Essential oils should be kept in small, dark-coloured, well-stoppered bottles, away from light and heat. Never keep the mixed oils for longer than 2 months as they will oxidise as soon as the essential oil has been added.

Essential oils to use include:
BASIL: refreshing
BERGAMOT: uplifting and relaxing
CALENDULA: healing and rejuvenating
CAMOMILE: relaxing and refreshing
CLARY SAGE: refreshing and said to be an aphrodisiac
GERANIUM: refreshing and relaxing
JASMINE: soothing and relaxing
LAVENDER: refreshing and relaxing
LEMON: refreshing and stimulating
LEMONGRASS: refreshing and reviving
MARJORAM: warming
MELISSA: refreshing and reviving
ORANGE BLOSSOM: very relaxing
PATCHOULI: relaxing
ROSE: relaxing and calming
ROSEMARY: refreshing and toning
SANDALWOOD: relaxing

CHAPTER
XIII

TUSSIE-MUSSIES

There be some flowers make a delicious Tussie-Mussie
or Nosegay both for sight and smell.
JOHN PARKINSON, *Paradisius*, 1640

The first purpose of a tussie-mussie or nosegay of herbs was medicinal. Judges carried them as they walked to the courts to ward off contagious diseases, and this custom is carried on to this day. By Elizabethan times the language of flowers was well-known and small nosegays were given to convey lovers' messages. Ophelia's was a sad one:

There's rosemary, that's for remembrance; pray,
love, remember: and there is pansies, that's for
thoughts...
There's fennel for you, and columbines: there's rue for
you;
and here's some for me: we may call it herb-grace o'
Sundays:
O you must wear your rue with a difference. There's a
daisy:
I would give you some violets, but they withered all
when my father died.

In the mid-eighteenth century the traveller, Lady Mary Wortley Montague wrote to a friend telling her of how Turkish women sent messages by means of flowers and when her letters were published, this rekindled a whole new interest. Illustrated dictionaries of flowers were published and the meanings of flowers were even included in nineteenth-century gardening books. Victorian ladies took great pleasure in making tussie-mussies and had special plots in their gardens where they grew the flowers for them.

A posy need not just be sent to a lover. It can convey good wishes at weddings, christenings and birthdays, cheer the sick, or provide a reminder of your visit to friends when you have gone. Use a tussie-mussie to decorate the dinner table or put it on the dressing table of the guest room. Small labels can be tied on to indicate the meaning of the flowers, or you may not be concerned with the meaning, preferring instead to simply make a pretty gift.

What flower like you best in all this border, heere be faire roses, sweete violets, fragrant Prime Roses, heere be Gilly-floures, Carnations, Sops-in-wine, sweet Johns, and what may either please you for sight, or delight you with savour: loth we are you should have a Posie of all, yet willing to give you one, not that which shall looke best, but such a one as you shall lyke best.

Sixteenth century

MAKING A TUSSIE-MUSSIE

A tussie-mussie usually consists of herbs and flowers arranged in circles round a large central bud such as a rose or camellia.

Good flowers to use include: Bachelor's Buttons, Burnet, Camomile, Clove Pinks, Cowslips, Forget-Me-Nots, Heart's Ease, Honeysuckle, Lavender, Marigold, Marjoram, Mignonette, Mugwort, Nasturtium, Primrose, Sage, Savory, Thyme, Verbascum, Violets, Wallflowers, and Woodruff.

Good herbs to use include: Basil, Barberry, Dill, Lovage, Marjoram, Meadowsweet, Mints, Mugwort, Nasturtium, Rosemary, Sage, Savory, Southernwood, and Thyme.

The best time to gather the flowers is in the evening after the sun has gone down. Pick as long stems as possible and singe any that secrete a milky fluid by holding them over a candle for 10 seconds. Then soak all the stems in cold water overnight. Should you have to shorten the burnt stems when making the tussie-mussie, singe them again.

To be able to make several circles, the stems of the outside flowers need to be bent outwards. If they are brittle, wind florist's wire round them first. Secure the stems together with wire, taking care not to make it too tight. Then tie them round with a ribbon.

Using dried flowers

If you want a tussie-mussie to be a long-lasting gift, make it with dried flowers. Scent it by using a dropper to put essential oils in the stems and tie it with a ribbon that has been steeped in lavender or rose water or eau-de-cologne and then dried. Once made, put it into a brown paper bag and leave it for three weeks in a dark place. Then it is ready for giving.

THE MEANING OF FLOWERS

ACACIA: chaste love; secret love

AGRIMONY: thankfulness, gratitude

ALMOND, FLOWERING: hope

ALYSSUM, SWEET: worth beyond beauty

AMARYLLIS: pride; splendid beauty

ANEMONE, GARDEN: forsaken

ANGELICA: inspiration

APPLE BLOSSOM: preference

BACHELOR'S BUTTONS: celibacy

BALM: sympathy

BARBERRY: sourness of temper

BAY: I change but in death

BELL FLOWER, WHITE: gratitude

BLUEBELL: constancy

BORAGE: bluntness

BROOM: humility

CAMELLIA, RED: unpretending excellence

CAMELLIA, WHITE: perfected loveliness

CARNATION, RED: alas for my poor heart

CARNATION, STRIPED: refusal

CARNATION, YELLOW: disdain

CAMOMILE: energy in adversity

CHINA ROSE: beauty always new

CHRYSANTHEMUM, RED: I love

CLEMATIS: mental beauty

COLUMBINE: folly

COWSLIP: pensiveness; winning grace

DAFFODIL: regard

DAISY: innocence

DAISY, GARDEN: I share your sentiments

EGLANTINE: poetry; I wound to heal

EVERLASTING FLOWER: unfading memory

FENNEL: praiseworthy

FERN: sincerity

FLEUR DE LUCE: fire

FORGET-ME-NOT: true love

FRENCH MARIGOLD: jealousy

GERANIUM, IVY-LEAVED: bridal favour

GERANIUM, OAK-LEAVED: true friendship

GERANIUM, ROSE-SCENTED: preference

GERANIUM, SCARLET: comforting

HAWTHORN: hope

HIBISCUS: delicate beauty

HONESTY: honesty, sincerity

HONEYSUCKLE: the colour of my fate

HOUSELEEK: vivacity; domestic industry

HYACINTH, WHITE: unobtrusive loveliness

HYACINTH, PURPLE: sorrow

HYACINTH, BLUE: constancy

HYSSOP: cleanliness

IRIS: message

IVY: fidelity; marriage

JASMINE, WHITE: amiability

JASMINE, YELLOW: grace and elegance

JONQUIL: I desire a return of affection

LABURNUM: forsake; pensive beauty

LARKSPUR: lightness; levity

LAUREL: glory

LAVENDER: distrust

LILAC, PURPLE: first emotions of love

LILAC, WHITE: youthful innocence

LILY, WHITE: purity, sweetness

LILY OF THE VALLEY: return of happiness

LIME: conjugal love

LOVE-IN-A-MIST: perplexity

LOVE-LIES-BLEEDING: hopeless not heartless

MAGNOLIA: love of nature

MARIGOLD: grief

MARIGOLD, FRENCH: jealousy

MARJORAM: blushes

MEADOWSWEET: uselessness

MICHAELMAS DAISY: farewell

MIGNONETTE: your qualities are supreme

MINT: virtue

MUGWORT: happiness

MYRTLE: love

NARCISSUS: egotism

NARCISSUS, DOUBLE: female ambition

NASTURTIUM: patriotism

ORANGE BLOSSOM: purity and loveliness

OX EYE DAISY: patience

PANSY: thoughts

PARSLEY: festivity

PENNYROYAL: flee away

PEONY: shame; bashfulness

PEPPERMINT: warmth of feeling

PHLOX: unanimity

PINK, RED DOUBLE: pure and ardent love

PINK, RED SINGLE: pure love

PINK, VARIEGATED: refusal

POPPY, RED: consolation

PRIMROSE: early youth

PRIMROSE, EVENING: inconstancy

QUINCE: temptation

ROSE: love

ROSE, BURGUNDY: unconscious beauty

ROSE, CABBAGE: ambassador of love

ROSE, DAMASK: brilliant complexion

ROSE, DEEP RED: bashful shame

ROSE, DOG: pleasure and pain

ROSA MUNDI: variety

ROSE, MUSK: capricious beauty

ROSE, WHITE: transient impressions

ROSEBUD: pure and lovely

ROSEMARY: remembrance

RUE: repentance, grief

SAGE: domestic virtue

SNOWDROP: hope

SORREL: affection

SOUTHERNWOOD: jest, bantering

SPEARMINT: warmth of sentiment

STOCK: lasting beauty

SWEET BASIL: good wishes

SWEET WILLIAMS: gallantry

TANSY: I declare war against you

THYME: activity

TUBEROSE: dangerous pleasures

VALERIAN: an accomodating disposition

VERVAIN: enchantment

VIOLET, SWEET: modesty

WALLFLOWER: fidelity in adversity

WORMWOOD: absence

YEW: sorrow

ZINNIA: thoughts of absent friends

SCENTED TOYS, PAPERS AND INKS

TOYS FOR CHILDREN

Fragrant herbs are not just for adults, indeed they need not only be kept for human beings! Children love scented things and herb-filled toys for puppies and kittens help to keep fleas away, besides being playthings.

For making childrens' toys, cut out shapes such as dolls, teddies, cats, dogs or rabbits. Keep the shapes simple, cut two the same and remember to leave ½ inch (1.5 cm) seam allowance all round. If the toys are to be stuffed completely with herbs, remember that it will be difficult to wash them, so use a strong, cotton material of a fairly dark colour. If you feel that washing will be necessary, make two more shapes of plain muslin to go inside an attractive outer cotton covering. The covering can then be removed and washed without disturbing the contents. If you find making the shapes difficult, some large stores sell cut-out toy patterns.

Put your shapes, right sides together and sew all round the edge, leaving a convenient-sized gap for turning and stuffing. Snip into all the curves, turn and press. Put in your herbs and sew up the shape by hand.

If you have stuffed muslin shapes to fit inside an outer cover, remember that they will be fairly stiff once full of herbs. It is therefore best to machine round half the outer cover, ease it round the filled muslin, and sew up the rest by hand.

Besides simple toys for toddlers you can make tiny toys to be hung by ribbon from a cot. Filled with a sleep pillow mixture they make an ideal present for a restless baby. The more it is touched and played with, the more likely it is to emit its relaxing scent.

Pretty, padded nightdress cases are always a favourite with children. Decorate them with patchwork patterns or appliqué, or make them into animal shapes. Slip into them two large, flat sachets of sleepy time herbs.

TOYS FOR ANIMALS

CAT MIXTURE

2 oz (50g) catmint
½ oz (15g) wormwood
(this keeps away fleas)
2 tbsp lemon verbena
This should fill a sachet
for the cat's bed, besides
one small mouse.

For cats, choose the herb catmint. They love it, rolling all over it in the herb garden and rubbing up against anything that contains it when dried. Gerard, in 1636, said of it: 'cats are very much delighted herewith; for the smell of it is so pleasant unto them, that they rub themselves upon it, and wallow or tumble in it, and also feed on the branches and leaves very greedily.'

Make cat toys in muslin bags with washable covers. Calico is a good material to use, or another strong cotton, and a simple mouse is the most popular shape. If you make a tail for it, sew it on strongly as this is always the first thing to come off.

Dogs do not care for catmint, and other sweet scents rarely attract them. However, a small sachet or toy filled with dried rue and placed inside their basket will help to keep away fleas. Make it bone-shaped, cat-shaped, lamb-chop shaped or whatever you think appropriate.

NOTEPAPER

Scented notepaper can be kept for your own use and it also makes a pretty gift. Buy a box of flower decorated notepaper, open it, and between the leaves put several small, flat sachets of any dry pot-pourri or sweet bag mixture that you think suitable. Seal the box with clingfilm and keep it for three months before opening.

INK

Scented ink will give a delicate, intangible fragrance to your personal letters, a fragrance that will waft out as soon as the envelope is opened and that will linger mysteriously over the pages.

Ink has its own scent so it is best to use herbs that have a strong fragrance such as lavender, rosemary, lemon verbena or hyssop. Use them dried for the best effect.

LAVENDER INK

½ oz (15g) dried lavender flowers

6 tbsp water

1 small bottle ink

Crush the lavender and put it into a saucepan with the water. Bring them to the boil and simmer for about 30 minutes or until you have 2 tablespoons brown, opaque liquid left. Strain, pressing down well. Mix the liquid with the ink.

LEMON VERBENA INK

1 oz (25g) dried lemon verbena

4 fl oz (125 ml or ½ cup) water

1 small bottle ink

Make as for lavender ink, simmering for 45 minutes or more if necessary.

HYSSOP INK

Use method for lemon verbena ink but substitute 1 oz (25g) dried hyssop.

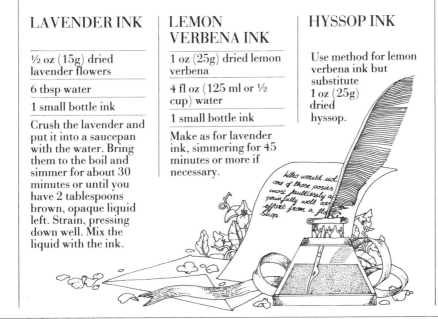

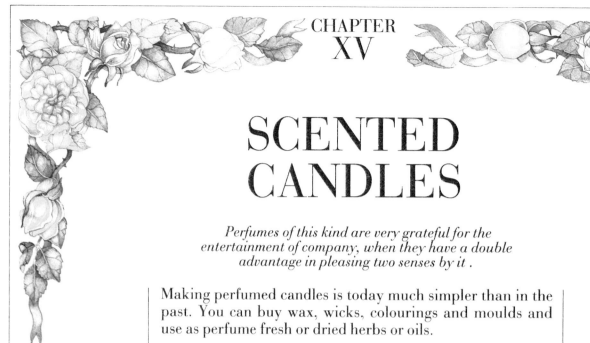

CHAPTER
XV

SCENTED CANDLES

Perfumes of this kind are very grateful for the entertainment of company, when they have a double advantage in pleasing two senses by it .

Making perfumed candles is today much simpler than in the past. You can buy wax, wicks, colourings and moulds and use as perfume fresh or dried herbs or oils.

Wax

Paraffin is the main candle wax used today. It is white and translucent, but used on its own will drip too much while the candle is alight. To prevent this, ten per cent of its weight of stearin is added to it. This is made from natural animal and plant oils and, like the paraffin wax, is white and odourless. Stearin mixed with paraffin wax also helps to distribute dyes and makes the candles easier to unmould.

Beeswax can be used alone or can be mixed with paraffin wax. It is soft and supple and burns steadily with a honey fragrance. When untreated it is an ochre colour which must be remembered when using dyes.

Scents for candles

A bunch of strong scented, fresh herbs, such as rosemary, lavender, lemon verbena or hyssop can be immersed in the

Making Scented Candles

Dried charcoal made of the branches of willow, an ounce; wood of myrrh, storax, calamite and aloes, of each an ounce and a half; of labdanum an ounce; of amber and musk of each seven grains [7 pinches]; oil of spikenard two ounces; spirit of wine; wherein gum tragacanth is dissolved, two ounces, beeswax four ounces. Make these by a gentle heat so soft that you may rowl them up like small candles over a cotton wick. And when you see your time, light one or more of them, and they will give a tolerable good light and perfume the place with a very pleasing odour; but if they give not light enough for the entertainment, you may set common candles amongst them, and these burning by the bedside of a sick person will be a great refreshment to the fading or drooping spirits.

MRS C.F. LEYEL, *The Magic of Herbs*, 1926

melted wax and left at a temperature just below 180°F, 75°C for 45 minutes. This will give a very soft fragrance.

Dried herbs can be mixed into the melted wax. The finished candle if not dyed, will have a translucent, grey-green colour, flecked with herbs. The scent, when burning, is very fresh.

Candle wax can also be perfumed with flower oils. Ordinary essential oils, either bought or of your own making, may not distribute evenly throughout the wax. It is best, therefore, to use special candle-makers' oils. Small amounts only are needed. Mix them into the stearin before adding it to the wax.

Dyes

Dye discs and dye powders can be bought from craft shops. If you cannot find them, wax crayons will work just as well. Only very small quantities of dye are needed. For example, for 1lb (450g) paraffin wax and 1 ½ oz (40g) stearin, you will need only one sixteenth of a small dye disc. Grate it into the melted stearin and stir into the wax when both are melted. To test if a dye is strong enough, drop 1 teaspoon of wax into a saucer of cold water and leave it to set. The final colour of the candle will look darker than your blob of wax as it will be more dense.

For a natural, orange-yellow dye, a small amount of turmeric can be added to the wax.

Wicks

Wicks can also be bought from craft shops. They are made from cotton yarn of varying thicknesses. Use a thicker wick for wider diameter candles. Candles made from beeswax also need thicker wicks. Candles with a high proportion of paraffin wax need only thin wicks. Paraffin mixed with beeswax of a higher proportion than normal of stearin need medium-sized wicks.

Moulds

Special candle-making moulds can be bought from craft shops, and these are the best to use as they have pointed tops which allow better burning. They are made of a transparent plastic, pliant rubber or metal.

You can also improvise moulds from many household items such as yoghurt and cream pots, tin cans and cardboard tubes. Punch holes in the bottom of yoghurt pots and cans for the wick. Cover the ends of cardboard tubes with card discs, well sealed and with a hole punched through the centre. When using scented oils, remember that they damage plastic moulds. This does not matter if you are using throw-away yoghurt cartons, but do not use oils with bought plastic moulds that you will want to use again.

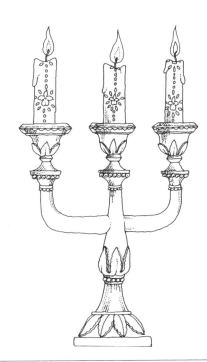

Before melting your wax, measure the total capacity of the moulds you intend to use. This prevents waste and incompletely filled moulds.

Preparing the moulds
Oil the moulds lightly with a good quality cooking oil. Push the wick through the bottom of the mould and bring it up to the rim. Tie it onto a cocktail stick or knitting needle. Place the stick or needle over the neck of the mould so the knot in the wick is in the centre. Keeping the wick taut, anchor the other end to prevent it from slipping back through the hole, using candle-makers' mould seal, plasticine or elastoplast. Completely cover the hole.

Bought molds have a small space underneath or a stand to enable the mold to stand upright without the knot making it tip to one side. If you are using a home-made mould with a flat base it will have to be placed on small raised supports (two cocktail sticks or pieces of wood will be fine). Place the prepared moulds in a dish, if possible as deep as the height of the moulds. Pour in cold water.

Temperature
Wax should be melted slowly. Use a double boiler or a casserole standing in a large saucepan of water and set them on a medium heat at first, lowering the heat to stop the water boiling. Wax is ready for use at 180°F, 75°C. It is best to use a thermometer, but if you do not have one take care never to let the wax start to bubble and use it while it is in a thin, liquid state.

Decorating candles with dried herb sprigs or pressed flowers
If you are going to decorate the finished candles, keep a little of the wax back. When you are ready to use it, remelt it in a double saucepan. Paint a little on the back of the flowers and stick the flowers to the candle. Paint over with more wax to secure them in position and give a translucent glaze.

Odiferous Candles Against Venom and the Plague

Take Labdanum three ounces, Storax ten drams [1 oz or 25g], Benjamin six drammes [½ oz or 15g], Frankincence an ounce and a halfe, Staechados two ounces, red Roses, Cloves, of each three ounces, Citron peele, Yellow Sanders, of each three drammes [¼ oz or 7g], Juniper berries halfe an ounce, Muske and Ambergreece, of each halfe a scruple: forme them into Candles with gum dragant dissolve in Rose water.'

The Charitable Physician, PHILIBERT GUIBERT, Physician Regent in Paris, 1639

BASIC METHOD

1 Prepare the moulds.

2 Put the wax into a double boiler and melt it. If you are using a bunch of fresh herbs for scent, add them to the melted wax, bring the temperature to 180°F, 75°C and keep it there for 45 minutes. Remove the herbs before adding the stearin.

3 Put the stearin into a small double boiler and melt it. This will take less time than the wax. If using dye discs of wax crayons, melt them with the stearin. Mix in the scented oil.

4 When the wax has melted and reached a temperature of 180°F, 75°C, mix in the stearin. If using powdered dye, sprinkle it in evenly and mix well. If using chopped herbs, mix them in at this point.

5 Pour the mixture into the moulds.

6 Leave the candles for about 10 minutes. If depressions start to form round the wicks, top up with more melted wax.

7 Leave the candles for 5 hours. To remove the candles from the moulds, pull on the cocktail stick or knitting needle, using it as a lever. If the candles will not come out, dip them briefly into hot water.

8 Leave the candles to cool if you have used hot water.

9 Trim the wicks. Flat-topped candles made in improvised moulds can be carved into pointed shapes using a knife dipped in hot water.

10 Polish the candles with cotton wool which has been dipped in vegetable oil

11 When you have used all the wax that you need, tip out any remainder while it is still liquid (not down the drain!). Pour boiling water into the pan and scrub vigorously with a long-handled brush. If you decide to take up candle-making as a hobby, keep special pans for it.

BEESWAX AND HONEYSUCKLE CANDLES

This will make candles of a total volume of 1 ½ pints (850 ml). The beeswax gives a natural, honeyed flavour to the bought oil. However, if you cannot obtain it, 1 ½ lb (675g) paraffin wax can be used with the same amount of stearin. The finished candles are a creamy yellow colour.

12 oz (350g) natural-coloured beeswax

12 oz (350g) paraffin wax

2 ½ oz (65g) stearin

6 drops honeysuckle candle perfume

pinch ground turmeric

Prepare the moulds. Put the beeswax and paraffin wax into a double boiler and melt them on a low heat. This takes about 20 minutes. Melt the stearin. This takes about 5 minutes. When the oil has reached 180°F, 75°C, sprinkle in the turmeric. Add the perfume to the stearin. Stir them into the wax. Mould, set and finish as in basic method.

LAVENDER CANDLES

This will make candles of a total volume of ¾ pint (425 ml)

12 oz (350g) paraffin wax

1 ¼ oz (35g) stearin

1/8 tsp finely-grated purple dye disc (enough only to make a light mauve)

1 oz (25g) dried lavender flowers

Prepare the moulds. Melt the wax in a double boiler. Melt the stearin with the dye. Stir the lavender flowers into the wax. Stir in the stearin. Mould, set and finish as above.

WILD THYME CANDLES

This will make candles of a total volume of ¾ pint (425 ml)

12 oz (350g) paraffin wax

1 ¼ oz (35g) stearin

1/8 tsp finely-grated pink dye disc (enough only to make a very pale pink)

1 oz (25g) dried wild thyme

Make as for lavender candles.

HYSSOP CANDLES

This will make candles of a total volume of ¾ pint (425 ml)

12 oz (350g) paraffin wax

1 ¼ oz (35g) stearin

1/8 tsp finely-grated green dye disc (enough only to make a pale green)

1 oz (25g) dried hyssop

Make as for lavender candles

WILD THYME AND PENNYROYAL CANDLES

Adding 2 tablespoons dried pennyroyal to the wild thyme makes the candles smell even more like chalk hills in summer.

CHAPTER
XVI

THE FRAGRANT GARDEN

I know a bank where the wild thyme blows
Quite o'er canopied with luscious woodbine,
With sweet musk roses and with eglantine.

SHAKESPEARE, *A Midsummer Night's Dream*

The delights of walking and sitting in a fragrant garden have been enjoyed since ancient times. Sweet-scented plants were grown by both the Greeks and the Egyptians and the Greeks planted beds of herbs outside their doorways so the sharp, clean, scents would waft inside.

The gardens of the ancient East were full of shrubs and trees which provided both rich scents and shade to sit in.

The Romans learned about scents and gardens from the Greeks and they took their knowledge all over Europe, growing herbs and flowers round villas and town houses.

In Anglo-Saxon times, herb lore and gardening were left mainly to the monks, but by the fourteenth century most manor houses and castles had fragrant gardens and arbours where knights and their ladies could walk, dance and engage in 'courtly love'.

And where the marjoram once, and sage and rue,
And balm and mint, with curled-leaved parsley grew,
And double marigolds and silver thyme,
And pumpkins 'neath the window used to climb;
And where I often, when a child, for hours,
Tried through the pales to get the tempting flowers:
As lady's laces, everlasting peas,
True-love lies bleeding, with the hearts at ease:
And golden rods and tansy running high,
That o'er the pale top smiled on passer-by;
Flowers in my time which everyone would praise,
Though thrown like weeds from gardens nowadays.

JOHN CLARE. c.1800

After the Wars of the Roses brought peace to England, more people had time to enjoy the scents of flowers and herbs, and by Elizabethan times every garden was a fragrant garden. It was most likely to have been laid out in knots, or geometric designs, often reproducing a design on the owner's house, and bordered with low hedges of fragrant herbs such as rosemary and lavender: 'It is a commendable and seemly thing to behold out of a window, many acres of ground well tilled and husbanded...yet more fair to behold delightful borders of lavender, rosemary, box and such like.'

In the seventeenth and eighteenth centuries, fragrant flowers and herbs were to be found in every cottage garden and in the more formal gardens of the large country houses, often cared for by the lady of the house. Victorian ladies, too, loved their gardens.

By the end of the nineteenth century, however, gardeners started to care for the appearance rather than the scent of their flowers.

In a mechanical, chemical world, we nearly forgot how beautiful a scented flower garden could be, but now we are beginning to realise its value once again. With the knowledge of all the old gardening writers before us together with the best of modern expertise, we ought to do well.

ROSES

First of all the rose, because its breath
Is rich beyond the rest, and when it dies
It doth bequeath a charm to sweeten death.

Probably the oldest known rose is *Rosa gallica*.

The Red Rose or the Apothecary's Rose, (*Rosa gallica officinalis*).
Other varieties: *Rosa mundi*, 'Belle de Crècy', 'Camaieux' 'Old Velvet' or 'Tuscany'.

The White Rose (*Rosa alba*)
Some varieties: *R. alba semi-plena*, *R. alba maxima*, 'Great Maiden's Blush', 'Celestial', 'Great Double White' or 'Jacobite Rose'.

The Musk Rose (*Rosa moschata*)
Hybrid musk roses: 'Felicia', 'Penelope', 'Buff Beauty', 'Moonlight', 'Cornelia'.

The Cabbage, Provence, Great Damask, or Holland Rose (*Rosa centifolia*)
Some varieties: 'Chapeau de Napoleon', 'Fantin Latour', 'Tour de Malakoff'.

THE MOSS ROSE (*Rosa centifolia muscosa*)
Some varieties: 'Blanche Moreau', 'Old Pink Moss', 'General Kleber', 'Henri Martin', 'William Lobb' or 'Old Velvet Moss'.

THE DAMASK ROSE (*Rosa damascena*)
Some varieties: 'Mme. Hardy', 'Alvilde Lees-Milne', 'Celsiana', 'Omar Khayam', 'Quatre Saisons'.

CHINA ROSES (*Rosa chinesis*)
Some varieties: *R. chinensis mutabilis*, 'Cecile Brunner', 'Cerise Bouquet', 'Bloomfield Abundance', 'Old Blush' or 'Common Blush'.

BANKSIAN ROSES (*Rosa banksiae*)
Best varieties: *R. lutescens*, 'Lutea'.

BOURBON ROSES
The first was a hybrid of *R. indicax* and *R. gallica*.
Some varieties: 'Boule de Neige', 'Mme. Isaac Pereire', 'La Reine Victoria', 'Adam Messerich', 'Zephirine Drouhin', 'Louise Odier', *R. eglanteria*, 'Manning's Blush', 'Janet's Pride', 'Sweet Brier'. Hybrids of 'Sweet Brier': 'Lady Penzance', 'Meg Merilles'.

RAMBLING ROSES
The Incense Rose: *R. Primula*.

'Blanc Double de Coubert' and 'Rosené de l'Hay': varieties of *R. ungosa*.

The Evergreen rose: *R. sempiverens*, 'Seliate aec perpetué', 'Adeleide d'Orleans'

'Goldfinch', 'Rambling Rector', or 'Shakespeare's Musk': varieties of *R. Multiflora*.

'Kiftsgate': *R. silipes*.

'The Burnet' or 'Scotch Brier': *R. pimpinellisolia*.

I think nothing can be more delightful than to throw open your window, and to inhale a refreshing odour from growing flowers when they are swept over by a balmy breeze.

MRS EARLE,
Pot-pourri from a Surrey Garden,
1905

Roses have never changed from the beginning of the world, and they have constantly created pleasure to this moment.

HELEN MILMAN,
My Kalendar of Country Delights,
1903

OTHER FRAGRANT FLOWERS

PRIMROSE (*Primula vulgaris*)

COWSLIP (*Primula veris*)

VIOLET (*Violet odorata*)
Cultivars: 'Coeur d'Alsace', 'Nellie Britton'

WALLFLOWER (*Cheiranthus cheira*)
Old names: Stock gilly-flower, wall-gillofloure, yellow stocke-gillofloure, Winter gillofloure

CARNATIONS (*Dianthus*)
'Dicker Clove', 'Bookham Perfume', 'Cherry Clove', 'Lavender Clove', 'Pamela Thain', 'Robin Thain', 'Oaken Fragrance'.

PINKS (*Dianthus*)
'Mrs Sinkins', 'Doris', 'Charles Musgrave', 'Loveliness'.

GILLFLOWERS (*Dianthus caryophyllus*)
Old names: Julian, Jove's flower, Tuggies, Gran' Père, gilly flower, Clove July flower, soppes-in-wine

SWEET WILLIAMS (*Dianthus barbatus*)

HELIOTROPE (*Heliotropium peruvianum*)

SWEET PEAS (*Larythus odoratus*)

PEONIES (*Paeonia*)
Old Dark Red Peony: *P. officinalis rubra plena*, 'Marie Crousse', 'Duchesse de Namours', 'Sarah Bernhardt': *P. chinesis*

MARIGOLDS (*Calemdula officinalis*)

CROCUSES (*Crocus*)
Various scented varieties flower from Autumn to Spring: 'Saffron' *(C. sativus)*, 'Cloth of Gold' (*C. susianus*), *C. longiflorus, C. tomasinianus, C. persicum, C. cilium.*

That which above all others yields the sweetest smell in the air, is the violet.

FRANCIS BACON

Nothing carries me back to my childhood like a bunch of cowslips. They are soft and sweet, and young, and altogether happy.

HELEN MILMAN,
My Kalendar of Country Delights,
1903

PHLOX (*Phlox*)
White, pink, and mauve varieties (eg. *P. maculata*) have the stronger scent.

NARCISSI AND DAFFODILS (*Narcissus*)
Many are sweet-scented: 'Baby Moon', *N. trevithian, N. actea, N. poeticus recurrus.*

GRAPE HYACINTHS (*Muscari*)

HYACINTHS (*Galtonia*)
The paler ones have the sweetest scents: eg. *G. candicans.*

IRISES (*Iris*)
'Common Flag' (*I. germanica*), 'Sweet Flag' *(Acorus calamus), I. florentina, I. pallida dalmatica, Acorus calamus), I. florentina, I. pallida dalmatica, Acorus calamus variegatus.*

LILY OF THE VALLEY (*Convallaria majalis*)

LILIES (*Lilium*)
'Madonna' (*L. candidum*), 'Lily of Japan' (*L. auratum*), *L. henryi*

SCENTED GERANIUMS *(Pelargonium)*

ROSE-SCENTED: *P. capitalum, P. graveolens*

LEMON-SCENTED: *P. variegatum, P. crispum major*

VERBENA-SCENTED: *P. crispum monor*

PEPPERMINT-SCENTED: *P. tomentosum*

APPLE-SCENTED: *P. odoratissima*

EUCALYPTUS-SCENTED: *P. clorinda*

SPICED SCENT: *P. fragrans*

INCENSE SCENT: *P. quercifolium major, P. quercifolium minor* (the oak leaved geranium)

And the hyacinth purple, and white, and blue, Which flung from its bells a sweet peel anew Of music so delicate, soft and intense, It was felt like an odour within the sense.

SHELLEY

SHRUBS AND TREES

From the delightful perfume of the myrtle, the delicacy
of its blossoms, and the gloss green of its perpetual
foliage, it seems destined to ornament the forehead of
beauty.

HELEN MILMAN, *My Kalendar of Country Delights*, 1903

JASMINE (*Jasminium officinale*)

WHITE FORSYTHIA (*Abeliophyllum distichum*)

WINTER-SWEET (*Chimonanthus praecox*)

MEXICAN ORANGE (*Choisya ternata*)

HAWTHORN (*Crataigus monogyna*)

CLEMATIS (*Clematis*)
C. cirrhosa balearica, C. flammula, C. jouiniana.

HONEYSUCKLE (*Lonicera*)
L. fragrantissima, L. periclymenum ('The Old Woodbine')

TREE LUPIN (*Lupinus arborens*)

BUDDLEIA (*Buddleia*)
'Black Night', 'Royal Red', 'Peace', 'Fascination',
'Dartmoor'.

MAGNOLIA (*Magnolia*)
M. wilsonii, M. grandiflora

LILACS (*Syringa*)
'Common Lilac' (*S. vulgaris*), 'Double White' (*S. persica*).

WISTERIA (*Wisteria*)

BAY LAUREL (*Laurus nobilis*)

MYRTLE (*Myrtus communis*)

NIGHT SCENTED FLOWERS

The night has made a nosegay of the stars
Bound with astraying fragrance from the South.

The following flowers all smell sweeter and richer at dusk:

ROSES (*Rosa*)

HONEYSUCKLE (*Lonicera*)

JASMINE (*Jasminium*)

NIGHT SCENTED STOCK (*Matthiola bicornis*)

FORGET-ME-NOT (*Myosotis sylvatica*)

NICOTINIAS (*Nicotinia*)
The paler flowers have the stronger scent: *N. affinis* or *N. alata* ('The Tobacco Plant'), *N. sylvestris*, *N. suavolens*.

EVENING PRIMROSE (*Oenothera biennis*)

NODDING CATCHFLY (*Silene nutans*)

WILD EVENING CAMPION (*Lychnis vespertina*)

Many a perfume breathed
From plants that wake
when others sleep.

115

FRAGRANT HERBS

Herbs to grow against walls and trellises
ROSEMARY (*Rosemarinus officinalis*)
WORMWOOD (*Artemesia absinthium*)
LEMON VERBENA (*Lippia onites*)

Herbs to make low hedges
KNOTTED GERMANDER (*Teucrium chamaedrys*)
LAVENDERS (*Lavendula*) 'Old English' and 'Grappenhall' are tall, 'Hidcote', 'Dwarf Munstead' are smaller varieties.
COTTON LAVENDER (*Santolina incana*)
FRENCH MARJORAM (*Origanum onites*)

Herbs for the back of a border
BERGAMOT (*Monarda didyma*)
TANSY (*Tanacetum vulgare*)
COSTMARY (*Chrystanthemum balsamita*)
MUGWORT (*Artemisia vulgaris*)
JERUSALEM SAGE (*Phlomis fruticosa*)
RUE (*Ruta graveolens*) variant: 'Jackman's Blue'
SAGE (*Salvia officinalis*)
RED SAGE (*Salvia officinalis purpura*)

Herbs for the middle of a border
SOUTHERNWOOD (*Artemisia arboratanum*) also known as 'Old Man' or 'Lad's Love'
HYSSOP (*Hyssopus officinalis*)
WHITE HOREHOUND (*Marrubium vulgare*)
CATMINT (*Nepata cataria*)

Low herbs for the front of a border

MARJORAM (*Origanum*)

SWEET or KNOTTED MARJORAM (*O. majorana*)

GOLDEN MARJORAM (*O. aureum*)

WILD MARJORAM (*O. vulgare*)

POT MARJORAM (*O. Onites*)

THYME (*Thymus*): *T. aureus, T. erectus, T. frangissima, T. odoratus, T. herba barona.*

COMMON THYME (*T. vulgare*)

LEMON THYME (*T. citriodorus*)

WOODRUFF (*Asperula odorata*)

LEMON BALM (*Melissa officinalis*)

MINTS (*Mentha*)

SPEARMINT (*M. spicata*)

PEPPERMINT (*M. piperata officinalis*)

APPLEMINT (*M. villosa alopecuoides*)

GINGER MINT (*M. gentilkis variegata*)

SAVORY (*Satoreja*)

SUMMER SAVORY (*S. hortensis*)

WINTER SAVORY (*S. montana*)

SWEET BASIL (*Ocymum basilicum*)

Herbs for paths and lawns

PROSTRATE THYMES: *T. serpillus coccineus, T. doerfleri, T. pink chintz,* these are particularly suitable.

BASIL THYME (*Calamintha acinos*)

CORSICAN SAVORY (*Satureia rupestris*)

PENNYROYAL (*Menta pulegium*)

LAWN CAMOMILE (*Anthemis noblis treneague*)

INDEX OF INGREDIENTS

119

OLD-FASHIONED TERMS AND INGREDIENTS EXPLAINED

AIRING CUPBOARD: Cupboard enclosing hot-water tank where linen is kept and clothes dried.

AMBERGREASE/ AMBERGREECE: Old spelling for ambergris (q.v.).

AMBERGRIS: Substance obtained from Sperm whale and used as fixative. Sandalwood is a plant alternative.

APOTHECARY: Ancient equivalent of pharmacist.

BALM OF GILEAD: Half-hardy herb (*Cedronella triphylla*) with balsam-like scent for refreshing pot-pourris.

BAWLME: Balm or lemon balm.

BAY SALT: Coarse, dark salt produced by evaporating sea water in open pans under hot sun.

BENJAMIN: Old name for gum benzoin, a fixative.

BODKIN: Small, bone implement used for making eyelet holes in material.

BRODERIE ANGLAISE: White cotton with white embroidery round a pattern of holes.

BUTTERMILK: Liquid left in churn after butter-making.

CALCINE: To reduce to ashes.

CARMELITE WATER: Toilet water thought to have been made first by the Carmelite friars.

CASTILE SOAP: Rich, white soap originally imported from Spain.

CASTING BOTTLE: Small bottle with perforated top for sprinkling.

CIVET: Secretion obtained from Civet cat for use as fixative. Orris root or vetevier are plant alternatives.

COURTLY LOVE: Courtship involving complicated Mediaeval etiquette.

CROCK: Large earthenware container.

DECOCTION: Liquid made by boiling herbs in water.

DESSICANT: Substance which absorbs moisture.

ESSENCE: Essential oil (q.v.).

ESSENTIAL OIL: Plant substance imparting scent and curative properties.

FEN COUNTRY: Low-lying marshy land in Lincolnshire and Cambridgeshire, England.

FIRE PAN: Frying pan.

FIXATIVE: Substance which preserves volatile scents.

FULLER'S EARTH: Form of powdered clay. Available Chemists and drug stores.

GILLYFLOWER: Carnation.

GROSS: Coarse.

GUM DRAGON/GUM TRAGACANTH: Dried resin which swells and gels in water.

HERB GRACE: Rue.

HUSBANDRY: Farming.

INFUSION: Liquid made by steeping herbs in boiling water.

JESSAMY: Jasmine.

LABDANUM: Sticky substance with balsam-like scent obtained from the rock rose, *Cistus ladaniferus*.

LAVENDER SPIKE: Lavender (*Lavendula spicce*).

LIGNUM ALOES: Dried or powdered aloe; a desert plant with spikey flowers and a balsam-like fragrance.

LITMUS PAPER: Specially prepared paper (which can be brought in strips or rolls) to indicate acidity/alkalinity of a substance.

MASTIC: Gum or resin from bark of certain trees.

MAWDELIN: Ox-eye daisy.

MEAD: Strong alcoholic drink made from fermented honey.

MILDEW: Fungus disease which attacks plants.

MOP CAP: Cap made from gathered circle of thin cloth.

MUSK: Substance from underbelly of Musk deer.

MUSK CODS: Musk.

MUSLIN: Thin cotton cloth with coarse weave.

ORACE POWDER: Orris Powder.

PAGGLE: Cowslip.

PELLITORY: *Parietaria officinalis* - a bushy perennial herb with red stems and flowers.

PRECIPITATED CHALK: Powder made from limestone solution. Available from chemists and drug stores.

QUASSIA CHIPS: Bark of Quassia tree of South America. Available from herbalists and some chemists and drug stores.

SALLET OYL: Salad oil.

SALT PETRE: Potassium nitrate.

SALVE: Soothing ointment.

SEARCHED: Sieved.

SLEIGHT: Trick.

SPIKENARD, OIL OF/SPIKE, OIL OF: Essential oil of American plant, Spikenard or 'Old Man's Root'. Available from herbalists.

STEARIN: Ester of glycerol and stearic acid. A soft, opaque wax made from natural animal and plant fats.

STILLROOM: Room for drying and processing herbs and flowers.

STREWING: To cover floors with sweet-scented plants.

'SWEET JAR': Pot-pourri made by the 'wet' method.

SWEET JOHN: White Sweet William.

TINCTURE: Substance in solution in alcohol.

YELLOW SANDERS: Yellow sandalwood.

YLANG YLANG OIL: Oriental flower oil.

STOCKISTS USA

APHRODISIA
282 Bleeker St
New York
NY 10014
212-989-6440

One of the nation's largest suppliers of dried flowers, herbs, spices, essential and fragrant oils, and fixatives. Their products are distributed on a nationwide basis through leading retail stores, and you may also order from their catalogue. Write for information and to order catalogue.

SWEETHEART HERBS INC.
Box 12006
Austin
Texas 78711
512-385-6988

Large supplier of pot-pourri and aroma-therapy products, including dried flowers, herbs, spices, tinctures, fixatives, essential and fragrant oils, ginseng, and bark. Call or write for a mail-order catalogue.

ANGELICA'S HERB AND SPICE COMPANY
137 First Avenue
(St Mark's Place and 9th St)
New York
NY 10003
212-677-1549

Sells bulk herbs and spices, pre-mixed pot-pourri and individual herbal and floral ingredients, including roots, barks, essential and fragrant oils. Also carries beeswax and ingredients for making scented candles. Send 8 x 10 SAE for mail-order catalogue.

STOCKISTS UK

G. BALDWIN & CO
173 Walworth road
London SE17

CANDLEMAKER'S SUPPLIES
28 Blyth Road
London WC2

CULPEPPER LTD
28 Milsom Street
Bath
(0225) 25875

12d Meeting House Lane
Brighton
(0273) 27939

25 Lion Yard
Cambridge
(0223) 67370

Unit 11
Marlowe Arcade
Canterbury

24 Bridge Street
Chester
(0244) 317774

10 Swan Lane
Guildford
(0483) 60008

4 The Corn
Exchange Buildings
Cornhill
Lincoln
(0522) 45013

1 Cavern Walks
Matthew Street
Liverpool
051-236 5780

21 Bruton Street
Berkeley Square
London W1
(01) 629 4559

9 Flask Walk
Hampstead
London NW3
(01) 794 7263

No 8 The Market
Covent Garden
London WC2
(01) 379 6698

14 Bridewell Alley
Norwich
(0603) 618911

7 New Inn Hall
Street
Oxford
(0865) 249754

33 High Street
Salisbury
(0722) 26159

4 Market Street
Winchester
(0962) 52866

43 Low Petergate
York
(0904) 51654